James Kitchener Davies

Editors:

Meic Stephens

R. Brinley Jones

Advisory board:

Jane Aaron

Dafydd Johnston

Writers of Wales

James Kitchener Davies

M. Wynn Thomas

University of Wales Press

Cardiff 2002

© M. Wynn Thomas, 2002

British Library Cataloguing-in-Publication Data.
A catalogue record for this book is available from the British Library.

ISBN 0–7083–1724–3

All rights reserved. No part of this book may be reproduced, stored in a retrieval system, or transmitted, in any form or by any means, electronic, mechanical, photocopying, recording or otherwise, without clearance from the University of Wales Press, 10 Columbus Walk, Brigantine Place, Cardiff, CF10 4UP. Website: www.wales.ac.uk/press

The right of M. Wynn Thomas to be identified as author of this work has been asserted by him in accordance with the Copyright, Designs and Patents Act 1988.

Published with the financial support of the Arts Council of Wales

Typeset at University of Wales Press
Printed in Great Britain by Dinefwr Press, Llandybïe

Er cof am fy nhad,
William John Thomas (1905–1962), Ferndale,
un o fechgyn y Rhondda.

Contents

Preface — ix

Chapter I — 1
Chapter II — 23
Chapter III — 45
Chapter IV — 67
Chapter V — 86

Notes — 94
Select Bibliography — 96
Index — 104

Illustrations

Illustrations 2–6 and 8 reproduced by permission of J. Kitchener Davies's family. Number 1 reproduced by permission of Manon Rhys and T. James Jones. Number 7 reproduced by permission of Dafydd Roberts.

1. '... a glade of tall trees —
   pines and tall larches — to break the cold wind,
   the wind from the north.'
   (*Sŵn y Gwynt sy'n Chwythu*, tr. Joseph Clancy) — 2

2. Kitchener with his brother Tom and sister Letitia (Tish), 1929. — 9

3. Kenry Street, Tonypandy, *c.*1928. — 21

4. The Pandy Players (Cwmni Drama'r Pandy), who performed *Cwm Glo* in 1935. Among the cast are the author, centre front; to his right, his sister, Tish Harcombe; to his left, Kate Roberts; centre back, his future wife, Mair Rees; to her left, Morris Williams, Kate's husband. — 30

5. Bethania Chapel, Llwynypia, 15 April 1940. Standing in the foreground, second from the left is Hannah, Kitchener's stepmother and behind her is Thomas Davies, his father. — 51

6. Mair and Kitchener, with, from the left, Megan, Manon and Mari, on holiday at Pantyfedwen, Borth, Ceredigion, 1951. — 71

7. With Gwenallt (David James Jones) at the Plaid Cymru Summer School, Dyffryn Ardudwy, 1949. — 88

8. James Kitchener Davies. This photograph was used on Plaid Cymru leaflets during the 1950 and 1951 General Elections in the Rhondda West constituency. — 91

Preface

James 'Kitchener' Davies is a seminal figure in the history of Welsh-language culture in the twentieth century. A charismatic character of boundless energy, he was a redoubtable political activist whose exploits earned him legendary status, celebrated a few years ago in the Ysgol Gyfun Rhydfelen stage production simply entitled *Kitch*. And he was also a writer of major importance, who produced three classics in *Cwm Glo*, *Meini Gwagedd* and *Sŵn y Gwynt sy'n Chwythu*, each of them experimental, controversial works that excited immense public attention in their day, and all of them works that have been out of print for many years. A volume concurrent with the present study will make them available again, and will set them, for the first time, in the context of Kitchener's many other writings – his autobiographical essays, his writings on drama and theatre, his political analyses, his commentaries on international affairs, his newspaper columns, his religious meditations. To list them is to be made newly aware of the range and diversity of Kitchener's talents as a writer, as well as a political and cultural activist.

For Kitchener Davies there could be no separation of culture from politics, particularly given the Welsh situation. An attempt has accordingly been made in the present study to convey the integrated, complex character of his life, thought, actions and writing. A man who identified so passionately with place needs, himself, to be 'placed' as exactly as possible if he is to be properly understood. Consequently, this study endeavours to explore his relation to rural Cardiganshire and industrial Glamorgan, to Welsh-language and to English-language Wales, to his own times and to ours. But above all, it seeks to re-examine Kitchener Davies the writer and artist, and to rescue him from the ravages of the very legend that has so far secured his popular reputation.

There is a sense in which Welsh Kitch has become Welsh kitsch; in which a comfortable, affectionate familiarity with a 'known' public identity, and the adoption of an 'assumed' name as the brand name of a potent form of cultural politics, prevents us from recognizing any longer the turbulent originality of Kitchener as a writer, the dimension of privacy to his work, the troubling and troubled nature of his gifts. After all, he was born plain James Davies, and known all his life to his immediate family as 'Jim'. The tendency has been to read his creative writings in the light of his politics. The time has surely come to read his politics in the light of his writings, having first placed his writings in a proper relationship to his intimate as well as his public self. This year (2002) marks the centenary of James 'Kitchener' Davies's birth, and the fiftieth anniversary of his premature death. It would therefore seem to be an appropriate occasion to read him again, and to read him differently.

While in no way wishing to associate the following people with my own revaluations of James Kitchener Davies I am very grateful to them for their assistance and encouragement while I was preparing this volume: Mr Cennard Davies and Mrs Mary Davies, Mr Tom Davies (Derlwyn, Tregaron), Professor Hywel Teifi Edwards, Mrs Astrid Hughes, Mr Glyn James and Mrs Hawys James, Dr Wyn James, Professor Ceri Lewis, Ms Barbara Prys-Williams, Dr Rhian Reynolds, Professor Meic Stephens, Dr J. F. Turner, and the late Dr J. Russell Stephens. Among the libraries I visited, whose staff kindly advised me, were Carmarthen Public Library, the Salisbury Library at University of Wales, Cardiff, Swansea Public Library, University of Wales, Swansea, and the National Library of Wales. All unattributed translations within the text are my own. I also gratefully acknowledge the permission granted by Mr Gwynn Pritchard (at the time Head of Broadcast, Welsh Language) to consult BBC materials at the National Library of Wales, and I am appreciative of the opportunity I was given to draft part of this work in the form of the 1999 Sir Thomas Parry Memorial Lecture of the Honourable Society of Cymmrodorion. I also wish to acknowledge the value of Ioan M. Williams's Welsh-language study of Kitchener Davies in the *Llên y Llenor* series. I appreciate the support provided by the General Editors of this series and by Llion Pryderi Roberts and his colleagues at the University of Wales Press. My warm thanks go to my daughter, Elin Manahan Thomas for preparing the index. Above all, however, I am indebted beyond measure to the kindness, guidance and support provided by members of Kitchener Davies's family; most particularly his son-in-law, Rheinallt Llwyd, who so generously shared with me the materials he had gathered for a prospective critical biography of the writer, and Manon Rhys, Kitchener Davies's daughter, who along with her partner, T. James Jones, showed an extraordinary trust in the work I was doing and demonstrated an exemplary forbearance and tact in responding to the crude text I ended up producing. Diolch o galon ichi am eich cefnogaeth hael a'ch cymorth parod.

Chapter 1

The Tregaron landscape — the austere bareness of the surrounding hills; the Teifi, little more than a stream, making its innocent-seeming way through the wide flood-plain of the green valley; the forked tail of the red kite silhouetted against the sky as it soars nonchalantly over the road; the great bog of Caron, its peat afloat on a water bed, biscuit-colour in winter light but flecked with broad dark pools. It was here that James (Kitchener) Davies was born on 16 June 1902, and raised in a two-roomed 'clod house', whose primitive structure contrasted with the hedges of patiently interwoven ash, thorn and beech his father had planted to protect Y Llain and to define the geometry of its meagre ten acres of tiny fields. Gathered round in a close knit of neighbourhood were the farms whose names, echoing back over eight centuries, and more, bespoke an old culture that had shaped the very landscape – Y Dildre, Tanbryn, Derlwyn, Pont Ddafad – a rich tapestry of warm sounds that lapped Kitchener Davies in community.

Austerity, though, lay within sight across the valley, where the Calvinistic Methodist chapel of Llwynpiod was to impress upon the growing boy the naked eloquence of spiritually convinced souls and the intensity of a religious life still luminous with the afterglow of the great revivals of 1859 and of 1904–5. The chapel stood on Sarn Helen, the old Roman road, a reminder that in this region even the most distant past seemed still to have one foot in the present, like Henry Richard, a giant figure of the nineteenth century, whose statue dominated Tregaron square. It was a fitting place to commemorate the achievements of a native son, dubbed the 'Apostle of Peace', whose role as international arbitrator led to his being honoured as far afield as Geneva. Tregaron had a long and famous tradition of linking with other worlds. It was there

'... a glade of tall trees —
pines and tall larches — to break the cold wind,
the wind from the north.'
(Sŵn y Gwynt sy'n Chwythu, tr. Joseph Clancy)

that for two centuries the drovers used to gather strength in the taverns before driving their stock to markets then so distant that even the geese had to be shoed for that long, rough waddle. And it was from Tregaron that many, like James Davies's father and then the young man himself, took off for the foreign world of the coalfield society in the south Wales valleys.

The Rhondda landscape – the baldness of the tip-strewn hills, lower slopes furrowed by terraces of grey houses; the tangle of indistinguishable townships cluttering up the long valley bottom; the pits rooting a new cosmopolitan industrial community in coal; Pentre, Llwynypia, Porth, Tonypandy, Welsh names all for communities rapidly adopting English as their *lingua franca*. Here Kitchener Davies, arriving as a young man, spent the whole of his adult life. Here he preached, agitated, campaigned – in one word, fought. Here he died in 1952 and was buried in Trealaw's Llethr Ddu cemetery. Here, too, he wrote his three major works: *Cwm Glo* (1935), *Meini Gwagedd* (1946), *Sŵn y Gwynt sy'n Chwythu* (1952). The first is a play about the Rhondda, the second a play about the Tregaron area, and the third a radio poem about his lifelong attempt, as writer and as political activist, to bring these two seemingly irreconcilable communities into meaningful relationship. 'O Lwynpiod i Lwynpia; o Rydypandy i Donypandy'; his affectionate use of internal rhyme to link the two localities betrays an urgent concern to use poetry (in the broadest sense) as a social connective. For him, of course, the language for connection had to be Welsh, for in Welsh, alone, could the past speak to the present right across Wales, even in the Anglicized Rhondda. What it had to say was that Tregaron and Treorci alike were places where the ordinary people lived under oppression from a different, and largely foreign, class. Kitchener Davies felt he had not needed to come to the Rhondda to experience poverty or social exploitation, and he was scathing about those who insisted that in order to understand such conditions he needed to turn to the different language of English and learn the new political language of a purportedly 'international' socialism.

According to his sister, the first significant piece of work produced by Kitchener was a school essay written during the First World War, after he'd seen a fighter-plane, piloted by a young man from the area, take off from a local field. That movement from one world to another, instanced so graphically in his own life by the change from rural Welsh-speaking Tregaron to Anglicized industrial Rhondda, was always to be what moved him to write, and it made him a writer profoundly representative of a country being radically reshaped by demographic change and culture shift.

His was a migrant imagination in search of new grounds for stability. Indeed, his passionate engagement with the Rhondda experience was owing, in part, to his heightened, outsider's, awareness of what was *sui generis* about it. In his great final poem it is as contrasted with the self-protectedly enclosed society of rural Tregaron that Rhondda's streets seem defencelessly open to the storms of change. But a late essay ('Hallmarked') reverses the picture, implicitly contrasting the openness of the countryside with the turbulently crowded landscape of coalfield society:

> our V-shaped industrial valleys, like the Rhondda, condition social life. Leisure activities are driven indoors since there is little room for spacious parks and playing fields.
>
> It is possible that in these glens more square feet of floor space per head of the population are taken up by public houses, billiard halls, skating rinks, dance-palaces, clubs (political and non-political), cinemas, workmen's institutions and libraries, church and chapel class-rooms than is normal in more open towns and cities where outdoor activities can compete with advantage.
>
> Each kind of hall in its separate way is a hive of social intercourse and a centre of the play of intellect. (*Herald of Wales*, 15 December 1951)

The landmark sights and nodal institutions of this society could scarcely have been more different from those that had given him his early bearings. The hall-mark (to adopt his pun) of Kitchener's adult life was his restless effort to make this landscape his own by bringing it closer to home.

But where then was home? To say it was the Tregaron of his boyhood and youth would be altogether too simple and cosy an explanation of his vexed case. Better to suggest, ambiguously, that he bore his 'imagination's nesting ground'[1] in mind to the end of his days, since it was there he found the fullest measure of his soul. Paradise lost it may have seemed at times, but he also spoke of being branded, Cain-like, by it, and of its pursuing him, like fate. The way the place haunted him like a passion is apparent in his electrifying late essay, 'Adfyw', where recollecting is synonymous with convulsive reliving. Stirred though he had been as a man by social, political and religious ideas, it was childhood experience alone, he there confessed, that had got under his skin:

> It's on William Sanders and Dani'r Dildre, Marged Tanbryn, Herbi and Long John and the others that I ponder. Keeping vigil over a cow ready to calve, tracking otters in the Teifi meadows, feeling the tingle of hoarfrost on potato haulm in October, seeing a heron rise, smelling paraffin in the long-room prayer meeting, hearing the screech of

plover and curlew, and the chiller screech of Ann, poor thing, as she suddenly went mad in the middle of the bog – it's these that insist on coming back to life in me . . . ('Adfyw', *Poetry Wales*, p. 20)

What is evident in the original Welsh is how uniquely capable Kitchener was of using his local dialect to register what he felt about what he saw. In the Tregaron of his childhood he had come alive to the sensuousness of a language that seemed the natural language of an opulently sensual world. There were meadows where little belldrops of dew fell on the naked foot from every bladelet of grass; tiny frogs, wanly yellow, exploded into life under the even paler yellow of the sun; experienced walkers, navigating their way through wetness, bobbed about dry as a cork in a waterfall. Kitchener spent a lifetime in the Rhondda blessed and burdened by a wealth of redundant vocabulary capable of caressing every detail and nuance of country life into blazingly distinct existence. What was he to do with it? He could, and did, use it to conjure a lost world into being. He could, and did, use it to create for himself a home from home in language. But mostly he treated it with a reluctant wariness, afraid of dialect's power to divide Wales into mutually uncomprehending regions, and aware of its seductive power to act as the lying language of idyll, and as the debased patois of *hiraeth*. Such were the concerns he placed on record in his 1936 *News Chronicle* article on the 'Dialects Problem on the Welsh Stage'.

Bountiful Tregaron had certainly been to him, but it had also left him a disquieting legacy. Ann's screech is unnerving enough in itself, but becomes doubly so if we hear in it a mocking echo of the primal loss Kitchener suffered in 1909, about which it seems he may have been dumb to tell until the very end of his life. He was six when one night his mother, alone in the house with three small children, the youngest of whom was four, struggled to give birth for a fifth time – another baby having apparently been lost two years previously. It was so stormy that the swollen Teifi prevented a neighbouring farmer, roused by Kitchener's eight-year-old brother Tom, from reaching the doctor in time. After the funeral the three children were sent away to an aunt in Banbury, the very town to whose fair Tregaron dealers had sent their cattle in droves. The children presumably spoke no English (98.2 per cent of Tregaron spoke Welsh in 1901) and in England they obviously heard no Welsh, outside the home. Kitchener never wrote about this first experience of 'exile', but it is hard to believe he was not marked by it. It may account for the particular edge there was to his anger later at the economic hardship that sent young Welsh men and women to England in hordes, like so many drovers' herds. And it may also have significantly heightened his attachment, upon his return, to a Tregaron he could never again take for granted or regard as simply given. He had been schooled early in the need to integrate different social experiences, but the way circumstances had kindly' allowed him to do this – by absorbing Banbury into Tregaron – proved altogether more difficult to repeat years later when he unconsciously attempted it with the Rhondda now in place of the English town.

His father's example filled him in boyhood with ambiguous feelings about the traffic between countryside and industrial valleys, and about the possibility of integrating them into a satisfactorily whole experience. Driven to working underground in Blaengarw in order to enable his family to make ends meet, Thomas Davies returned to Tregaron only at Easter, in August and at Christmas time, those key dates in the farming calendar. But in 1911 the great Cambrian Combine strike, a significant event in the very different industrial calendar, allowed him to spend virtually the whole of the summer at home, to his son's delight. Excelling at hedging, fencing and all other forms of woodcraft, his father exhibited craftsman's skills typical both of his native rural community and of the industrial valleys where he worked underground as a carpenter. In his reminiscent newspaper essay, 'Fy Awr gydag Edward Frenin', Kitchener would later movingly reflect that every time he'd walked on wooden walkways through the bog to Sunday school in Llwynpiod chapel, and every time he'd gone courting by way of the wooden bridge over the stream, it had been his father's handiwork that had allowed him safe passage. Though a country boy in Tregaron, Kitchener had therefore been unconsciously dependent on skills honed underground in Blaengarw. It was a benign parable of the complex social and economic interdependence of two very different societies. But the relationship could also assume much more malign aspects, as was brought home to him in adolescence when it began to seem that he, too, was doomed to go down the pit.

From the beginning, then, Kitchener knew how directly and intimately economic circumstances affected people, a harsh fact of life that later put a hard edge on his cultural nationalism and prompted him to act the verbal bruiser in the rough-house of Rhondda's labour politics. Tregaron, a community of some six hundred people, had always been at the mercy of changing economic links the market town had with other regions. Down to the coming of the railway in 1866, the determining link had been simply and dramatically defined by the drovers' celebrated cattle trail to London. Thereafter the London connection – now maintained only by the dairy industry in which Kitchener's brother was to earn his living – became subordinate to Tregaron's growing links with south Wales. It began with the development of a woollen industry and hosiery trade to supply the new needs of an expanding coalfield, and Kitchener's grandmother was one of those who walked to Aberdare, knitting stockings as she went, to spend a period teaching in school. Simultaneously, the coalfield was recruiting a new labour force of miners and female servants from the rural areas. Kitchener's father worked underground and two of his mother's sisters went into service in the valleys. Gradually a workforce that had begun by seeking temporary, migrant and seasonal labour found its permanent home in the south, as was to happen with Kitchener's family. At the same time, most of the hosiers ceased selling from Tregaron and moved down to establish drapers' shops in the densely populated industrial communities. Factors such as these account for the erosion of the rural population during Kitchener

Davies's lifetime. The population of Cardiganshire fell from 61,000 in 1901 to 53,000 in 1951, with the biggest drop, of 9.36 per cent, occurring during the very decade (1921–31) that saw Kitchener himself settling in the Rhondda.

It was the return from the Rhondda of Kitchener's Bodo (aunt) Mari, his mother's sister, that allowed the children to come back from Banbury to Y Llain. Though puritanically stern in her ways, a stickler for good morals and proper manners, she devoted herself to the family's welfare. By working together, they were able to make ends meet, although their meagre acreage was sufficient to support only two cows, a few hens and a couple of pigs. As Kitchener recalled in 'Adfyw', the cruelty of life first reached him in the squeal of a dying pig and the cry of a trapped hare. Since there were no horses on the farm, neighbours had to rally round to help at harvest time. Relations on both their mother's and father's side were also thickly dotted about the locality, and such a large extended family was of value in an area where kinship ties remained much stronger than those of class. As the social geographer, Emrys Jones, was to remark, 'In this the society is reminiscent of the great bogland which is so conspicuous a feature of the landscape; if you gently depress the bogland with your foot it sags only a little, but fully twenty yards away tall grasses will sway gently in response.'[2]

The names of the three Davies children were themselves an affirmation of family solidarities, since Thomas, the eldest, was so named after his father and paternal grandfather, Letitia (Tish, the youngest) after her paternal grandmother, and James after his maternal grandfather. Known in the family as Jim, and to the whole neighbourhood as Jim bach y Llain (little Jim of the Llain), he was sometimes teasingly called Kitchener by his father (who sported a fine Kitcheneresque moustache). The pet name came into its own at school, where it was used to distinguish him from the myriad other Davieses. Later in life it became a *nom de guerre*, defiantly claimed as his own by an anti-colonial Welsh nationalist and supporter of the peace movements who hated and despised everything the imperialist, war-mongering Lord

Kitchener with his brother Tom and sister Letitia (Tish), 1929.

Kitchener had stood for, but who fought as fiercely and fearlessly as he had done for his beliefs. Nowadays such a significant act of self-renaming would be regarded as a witty post-colonial comment on the imbrication of language and identity.

Although Kitchener's mother was given an Anglican burial in the parish churchyard, he and his siblings attended service and Sunday school at Llwynpiod Calvinistic Methodist chapel. Plainly visible from Y Llain, it seemed conveniently near, although it could actually be reached only after a two-mile walk around the intervening bog. The emotional fervour of the sermons, the intellectual fervour of the Sunday school sessions, and the soul-scouring confessions of the *seiat* meetings all left a profound mark on his sensibility and spirit. A stronghold of the Calvinist faith, and long renowned for its devoutness, the town of Tregaron, only slowly recovering from revival fever, was capable of seeming comically solemn. As a little boy, Kitchener found a verse suitable for reciting in chapel printed on a jampot bought in a town where 'Praise the Lord' was still blazoned in many a shop window. On the other hand, the future writer in him benefited immeasurably from growing up in a community whose earthy quickfire Welsh was periodically changed by Biblical idioms and phrases into a grand diapason of serious eloquence. The printed word, too, had scarcity value. Unable to work or play on Sundays, when even the parish pump would be padlocked by pious Sabbatarians, the children opened the few religious comics they were allowed like magic casements. Best of all, though, were the home-made entertainments involving language games. No wonder that in Kitchener's time the Tregaron area produced a whole generation of virtuoso talkers, poets and entertainers, some of whom became well-known radio performers. Wits, wags, wild improvizers and wilful fantasists, their talk swollen gently by the yeast of insobriety, they could be saboteurs of solemnity and anarchists of language. One of them was Cassie Davies, whose autobiography, *Hwb i'r Galon*, showed that her memory in old age was a riot of rhymes, proverbs, provocative tags, scurrilous chants, *penillion*, *englynion*, and all the marvellous verbal bric-a-brac of the by then long-lost world, of fireside get-togethers and *nosweithiau llawen*, she had shared with Kitchener Davies.

In his essay, 'Mossbawn', Seamus Heaney has recorded the importance to a poet of discovering early the oral literature that delights us by 'reflecting our experience [and that] re-echo[es] our own speech in formal and surprising arrangements' (p. 26). Kitchener Davies made that discovery in his Tregaron boyhood and it fed into his mature work. But he also discovered those 'home' truths concerning its darker self about which Tregaron kept silent, a silence he later made it his business to break. Mad Ann's screech from the bog came from such silence, and out of it, in part, Kitchener fashioned *Meini Gwagedd*. Another silence, much nearer home, was broken only when Kitchener learnt (probably at school) that Bodo Mari, when young, had given birth to an illegitimate son, who had been raised by her sister Ann as one of her own. This circumstance is addressed most directly in *Cwm Glo*, but in its widest ramifications it affected the way in which Kitchener the writer viewed the whole world of Wales and of human nature. And the final silence? This was the inner silence Kitchener kept the whole of his life about what the loss of his mother, and two other related losses, had meant to him inwardly. This was a silence he finally brought himself to break, as he was dying, in *Sŵn y Gwynt sy'n Chwythu*.

The Anglican background of the family reasserted itself in the choice of primary school, the children having daily to walk three and a half miles to the Church school in Tregaron. Although Kitchener appreciated the grounding in the Bible and the catechism he was given there, it was the move up to Tregaron County School that proved vital in his case. Opened only in 1897 with 98 pupils, and greatly expanded in 1909, the school was a powerhouse of social transformation. Elsewhere in the Wales of that pivotal period the elite county schools were, in effect, instruments of a social advancement that involved the production of a new class formation based on a kind of cultural colonization; the oral, socially transmitted indigenous culture was replaced by that of the literate, educated English middle class. In Tregaron, too, education at this level aimed to produce a new, professional class of cultural 'managers'. English was the medium of teaching, conveniently allowing some teachers to conceal the fact that their mother tongue was Welsh. The school was, however, fairly unusual in the respect it accorded the local 'native' culture. The result was that it produced a remarkable number of the most distinguished writers, scholars and intellectuals of Kitchener Davies's lifetime, as he proudly recalled in his *News Chronicle* piece 'Fine Lead for School Producers' (1935). And the key figure controlling this remarkable production belt became a key figure, too, in Kitchener's development as person and as writer.

By common consent, S. M. Powell was an inspirational teacher. He taught Welsh and English throughout the school, but History was his main subject. As an antiquarian he was fascinated by the local past, and as a trained historian he was equally fascinated by the links between local events and those of the wider world, links which he illustrated through such stimulating details as the piece of Tregaron beef that had appeared on the platter of the Black Prince in France. He had an eclectic appreciation of every kind of historical deposit, valuing local lore, oral tradition and legend as well as official historical records, while scrupulously maintaining a professional distinction between their respective functions and status. He encouraged his pupils to dig – literally in the case of Roman remains – into the deep past of their locality, and to relish its many layers. Beginning with the Bronze Age hill forts, they progressed to studies of the Second Augustan Legion, the Celtic saint Caron, down to local evidence of the traumatic social consequences of the change, in the wake of the 1536 Act of Union, from the old Welsh preoccupation with genealogy to the new English laws of inheritance.

Under Powell, Kitchener Davies developed that prophetic eye for the fateful history of the present which was to inform all his writing and all his political activity. And through him, Kitchener came to understand his own traits of personality and principle in terms of the precious and providential cultural legacy of his birthplace. His rooted hostility to war was akin to that of Henry Richard, the great 'Apostle of Peace'; his inclination towards Calvinism was part of the very spirit of place, since all the great founders of Welsh Methodism had close connections with Tregaron – Daniel Rowland's Llangeitho was only four miles distant, William Williams had regularly visited the town, Howell Harris had famously enthused a vast open-air congregation on the square outside the Talbot Hotel; and Kitchener's visceral political radicalism was cousin to that of the author of *Uncle Tom's Cabin*, Harriet Beecher Stowe, whose great, great grandmother had come from Tregaron. Important, too, was Kitchener's discovery of the true story of Twm Siôn Catti, that celebrated Welsh Robin Hood which the early nineteenth-century Anglo-Welsh novelist, T. J. Llewelyn Prichard, had invented if not out of thin air then on the basis of the flimsiest historical evidence. Thomas Jones, the 'original' of Twm, had been a noted Tregaron landowner, antiquary, genealogist and minor poet, and his distortion by Prichard must have seemed to Kitchener an instance of that cultural self-maiming that had happened throughout history whenever the Welsh had been induced to ape the English.

Two aspects in particular of S. M. Powell's contribution left an indelible mark on Kitchener as a youth; the debates that he organized and the plays based on local history he urged his pupils to plan. Powell turned their outline sketches into scripts which the youngsters then performed at the annual Christmas prize-giving ceremony. Kitchener later owed not a little of his redoubtable skills as political polemicist and public speaker, and his consuming interest in writing for the stage, to Powell's early ministrations.

The pride in Tregaron past and present that Powell inculcated in his pupils merged in Kitchener's case, as he matured intellectually, into an updated version of the dream of the redemption of (Welsh-speaking) Wales through the dictatorship of the *gwerin* (the cultured *Volk*). By the end of the nineteenth century this had come to be the dominant ideology of Nonconformist Wales and had been given sophisticated expression by notable scholar-writers such as O. M. Edwards. The first half of the twentieth century saw this ideology, in suitably modified form, infiltrating the thinking and policies of Plaid Genedlaethol Cymru – later known as Plaid Cymru. At the same time it was given a further new lease of intellectual life in the 'scientific' work of an important generation of Welsh sociologists, anthropologists and social geographers. Iorwerth Peate was one of the most influential of these figures, and Kitchener acknowledged a particular debt to his volume *Cymru a'i Phobl*. There, under the guise of dispassionate analysis of the socio-geographical features of the Welsh peninsula, Peate advanced the view that the heart, soul, or *nucleus* of Wales had long principally resided in the culture of its great, central upland 'plateau' that stretched all the way from Mynydd Hiraethog to the hills of Breconshire and Carmarthenshire. A corollary of this was his belief that those southern tongues of land containing the coalfield societies were the invitingly open gateways through which an invading foreign culture had poured. The obvious disadvantages, to put it no more strongly, of basing a political programme on such an inappropriate ideology when campaigning in the ethnically mixed Rhondda should surely have registered with a Kitchener whose sister, Letitia (Tish), herself married the Labourite son of an immigrant from Devon and a native of Cwmavon.

Although not, by his sister's account, the scholar Tish was at the County School, Kitchener was clearly destined for sixth form and university when a bombshell arrived. On one of his periodic returns from Blaengarw his father announced his intention of marrying a 'valleys' woman. He had hoped to take advantage of the break-up of the big landed estates during the First World War, to buy a bigger farm, but was foiled in this attempt by the steep rise in prices as big money moved in, again forcing many of Tregaron's traditionally small farmers to the wall. Thomas Davies was therefore forced back on his second option; he sold Y Llain – concerned neighbours buying back some of the most cherished possessions at auction so that they could be kept in the family – and moved south permanently to set up his new home in Blaengarw. It was, Kitchener confessed thirty years later, the biggest hurt of his life after losing his mother. The sale would effectively have sentenced him to a lifetime in the pits had not considerate teachers and relatives, knowing of his school record, persuaded his father to let him enter the sixth form. Nevertheless, he and his sister (his brother Tom having departed for London) both moved south with Bodo Mari to settle in the house she still owned in Kenry Street, Tonypandy, returning to lodge in Tregaron only during the school terms.

Fifteen years after the event, Kitchener published a short story entitled 'Y Llysfam' (The Stepmother) so startlingly closely modelled on the events surrounding the sale of Y Llain it seems permissible to regard it as an imaginative reworking of his real feelings at the time. Glyn is a young boy living on a smallholding and being raised, along with his brother and sister, by an aunt while his widowed father supports the family by working underground in the south. Failing one year to buy a bigger farm for his family from a large estate, the father shocks them by marrying a 'little woman' from the south without his relatives' knowledge – the news reaching them only after the wedding – and by making arrangements for the sale of the smallholding. Bitterness sets in on both sides and recriminations follow, but Glyn finds himself not blaming his father so much as the 'little woman', whom he has never even seen. Reasserting himself, his father seems determined to have Glyn work underground, but his aunt, although forced to move the family home to the Rhondda, succeeds in keeping the youngster at school in the old village, defraying all the costs involved herself.

For Glyn, the most devastating blow is the accidental discovery, in his father's coat-pocket, of a simple letter from the 'little woman' indicating what furniture in the old family cottage should be sold and what should be carried south to her. 'Why should this stranger lord it over what are my things and were my mother's?' he wonders (p. 251). It is 'y fenyw fach', the 'little woman', who comes to represent for him the break-up of the old home and the uprooting that turns him from a country lad into a town dweller. (In his late essay 'Adfyw' Kitchener admitted he could still recall, through his very feet, the sensation of first walking on hard pavements rather than over soft grass and earth.) Yet, the narrator of the story pointedly adds, all who know Glyn understand it was through this act of enforced exile that he became an internationally acknowledged author.

As it develops, the story works up to the note of melodrama that Kitchener was always to find it difficult to resist, except that in this case the melodrama seems to ring true to extremes of feeling in Kitchener's own psyche. The narrative cuts to Glyn on his deathbed, where he is tormented by a need to confess. He had nursed a grudge against his stepmother, concealing it in the dark recesses of his soul. One day, an opportunity came for him to offer her a lift in the sidecar of the motorbike he was about to ride over the mountain between one industrial valley and the next. The road was steep, its treacherous bends curving over precipitous drops, and the motorbike's engine sang sweetly. Indeed, the engine seemed to take on an independent life of its own, pistoning purposefully away, conditioning its rider to the new intoxicating rhythm of the perfect machine. But then the pistons started to sing a siren song of curses on the stepmother, a song irresistibly seductive to Glyn's soul, and the next thing he knew was that motorbike, sidecar, he and she had all plunged off the road and over the edge. He survived; she did not. The inquest had acquitted him of all blame, but years later, on his deathbed, he agonizes over the question he voices only to his friend:

> You have studied the new kind of thinking [i.e. psychoanalysis]. Tell me the truth. Do you think it could have been the secret power of the motorobike that drove me unbeknown to myself and made me a murd . . .? (p. 264)

'Y Llysfam' may not be the best of stories but its biographical relevance is so compellingly evident that perhaps a degree of caution is needed. Better, therefore, summarize the findings in the form of queries that indicate possibilities rather than of statements that suggest certainties. Did Kitchener, through the circumstances surrounding the sale of Y Llain, come to associate the south with the threat to (cultural) inheritance? Did it predispose him to think of Welsh-speaking Wales as culpably ready to sell out? Did his writing find its roots deep in psychic disturbances, such as the trauma of exile and the pain of having been betrayed and left by *both* his natural parents? How far did his Calvinistic sense of ingrained sin derive from difficulties he had in forgiving himself for so hating his stepmother? Was the anger he felt for 'the little woman' a displaced expression of the repressed anger he had felt ever since the death of his mother? How much was the combative energy he so famously showed in his tireless organizing and campaigning due to an underlying fear (voiced in the story) that he might resemble his father, who had been so disastrously afraid to face unpleasantness? And the association of the machine with the fear of losing individual moral responsibility – does this illuminate Kitchener's attitude towards the miners in their pits?

Even if all this is dismissed as idle psycho-babble, the concluding lines of 'Y Llysfam' seem to anticipate Kitchener's own dying gesture with uncanny accuracy. At his death, Glyn left one last play: 'In it he exposed his soul – and it is cruel; terribly cruel – it weighs a man down to the very floor' (p. 264).

Kitchener Davies left the County School to take what turned out to be a mediocre degree at the University College of Wales, Aberystwyth, where he then trained as a teacher. When he arrived at the college, still companionably based along 'the prom', student numbers had just dramatically risen from 250 to 1,100, as young soldiers flooded back into civilian life. The atmosphere was understandably heady with hope and hedonism, and the period was a remarkable one in the history of a college proud of its (strictly relative!) antiquity, and its status as the founding, and still supposedly principal, college of the University of Wales. Kitchener Davies was later to value the fact that the bicultural Welsh drama movement, which had attracted international attention during the opening decades of the century, could be dated back to its beginnings in 'Aber' in 1879, and that in J. O. Francis and D. T. Davies the college had produced two of its star writers. More important to Kitchener the college fresher, however, was the public notoriety of the institution during the war, following student protests that were led by a former undergraduate, D. J. Williams, who had moved on to Jesus College, Oxford, and that were bravely backed by a then young staff member, T. H. Parry-Williams. Outspoken in their criticism of militarism and imperialism, the students were in favour of the anti-colonial struggles of Sinn Fein and a rapprochement with the 'Hun'. These protests were prophetic in that they prefigured the way young Welsh intellectuals of Kitchener's generation were to give a new, cutting political edge to the liberal cultural nationalism of their elders, and were to make pacifism and anti-colonialism into core elements of their nationalist ideology.

For students such as Kitchener, there were giants in the land in those days, in the form of the leaders of what might be described as the second phase of development of the modern secular Welsh intelligentsia. During the first phase, great pioneers such as John Morris-Jones and Ifor Williams had standardized the Welsh language, analysing it philologically and systematically regulating its grammar. And they had done so whilst rediscovering, recovering and refurbishing a great literary tradition, stretching back well over a thousand years; a heritage of which a culturally colonized Wales had virtually lost sight. Figures of the second phase put these developments to startlingly creative use, thus instigating a remarkable renaissance of Welsh-language literature, while also extending, reinforcing and refining the scholarly work accomplished by the first generation. At the same time, the growing prestige of these new culture heroes, and their commanding intellectual achievements, made their relationship to the Nonconformist ministers who had been the respected leaders of the old order a difficult and, at times, a very stormy one.

T. Gwynn Jones and T. H. Parry-Williams, two of the most charismatic figures of the new intellectual dispensation, were amongst Kitchener's teachers. Respecting them both, he fell particularly under the influence of the former, remaining in literal and metaphorical conversation with him throughout his life. Particularly important to him were T. Gwynn Jones's inventive attempts to explore Welsh history by developing new literary genres formed through the fusion of poetry and drama. 'When it comes, some time, to assessing Welsh drama', he wrote in his 1949 essay for *The Torch*, 'it will be discovered, I would propose, that it is to T. Gwynn Jones that we are most indebted' (p. 15). At least as important to Kitchener in the long- as well as the short-term, however, was the unique performance culture created by the student body of that period. Crucial, here, was the fact that the leaders were not youngsters fresh out of school but veterans of the very grimmest kind of wartime service. Out for fun they understandably were, but there was much more to it than that. Through their fun they could demonstrate their dissent from a solemn Nonconformist culture whose influence on its young had proved so murderously effective; they could undertake their own cultural salvage operation, recovering, on modern terms, the spirit of a pre-Methodist culture that revelled in dance, ballad, folksong and fair; they could reaffirm the resilience of Welsh-language culture, by demonstrating its contemporaneity with cinema and the jazz age; in a spirit of mild carnival, they could mock their academic rulers and the rules of the education game that the economically and culturally disadvantaged Welsh had been taught to take so seriously as the means to social respectability and acceptance by the English. Student life was, then, not just a release valve but a kind of decompression chamber, allowing some of the students safe passage from British imperialism to a new-style Welsh nationalism. In this way, the University of Wales, primarily through its colleges at Aberystwyth and Bangor, was helping unawares to educate a generation of politico-cultural nationalists at much the same time that the Central Labour College in London was educating a generation of militant 'international' socialists. Kitchener Davies's political campaigns in the Rhondda were to bring the graduates of the one college into direct conflict with those of the other.

The undisputed star of the Aber show was Idwal Jones, a native of Lampeter, just a few miles south-west of Tregaron, who may reasonably be regarded as the founder of modern Welsh light entertainment and one of the originators of popular culture. He arrived in April 1919, after some four years' service in East Africa and periods of convalescence in fifteen hospitals, and for him aspects of the college scene must have seemed surrealistic. Even those students who were war veterans in their mid-twenties were forbidden to speak to women undergraduates, off college premises, after seven o'clock at night – a delicious, if frustrating, piece of absurdity that Idwal Jones made the central event of his pioneering musical comedy, *Yr Eosiaid* (The Nightingales).

Idwal Jones was a Prospero who conjured up a marvellous storm of entertainments, by which it seems Kitchener was caught up and swept away. ('Jim was always a bit of a flirt,' his sister Tish fondly remembered.) Popular tunes were hijacked and Welsh words set to them; parodies of serious texts were produced; sketches were written, reviews performed, limericks improvised; academic worthies were affectionately debunked; mock eisteddfodau were held. At this distance it all seems poignantly innocent – little more than Nonconformity sedately letting down its hair – but for Kitchener's generation of students it was an exciting cultural revolution, and it provided Kitchener himself with a series of important insights that were to govern his writing career.

From that world of festival over which Idwal Jones presided like a genial Lord of Misrule, Kitchener learnt many things; that amateur productions could reasonably aspire to professional standards; that a group of performers could make an excellent cell of cultural and political activists; that dramatic performances could alter minds and change lives – the lives both of the participants and of their audience; that writers for the stage needed to feel on their pulses what worked and what did not; that the *Sturm und Drang* of theatre made it an incomparable forum for impassioned debate; that, in dramatic as well as in social terms, honesty could be the best policy; that a writer for the stage had to adopt a flexible approach to genre, language, idiom; that in writing for the theatre, as in performing on stage, one could not stand still for long; that the audience for a performance had to be identified, clearly envisaged, and always, always borne stubbornly in mind.

Kitchener took with him a great deal he had learnt at Aberystwyth when he left college to teach in the Rhondda. He would never be above lacing his speeches with humour or enlivening his campaigning with pranks. Above all, perhaps, he took with him a taste, which he never lost, for intellectual companionship and for creative collaboration. In 'Staff Ysgol', a piece he wrote for *Yr Athro* not long after becoming a teacher, he ruefully

Kenry Street, Tonypandy, c.1928.

admitted there was nothing more disillusioning than failing to find in a school staffroom the kind of mutuality of interest and reciprocity of thinking one had grown to love as an undergraduate. In one respect, the Welsh-language sub-culture of the Rhondda in which he so vigorously participated, and whose members seemed to the dominant socialist culture to constitute a sinister fifth column, provided Kitchener with a substitute for the life he had led in college. He certainly needed to provide himself with some kind of life-support system, because the move to the Rhondda was for him almost a step into the unknown. Thirty years later, he could still recall it vividly in his radio essay 'Adfyw', and could still wonder what it all meant:

James Kitchener Davies

As I look back over the whole journey through the wilderness, I have come to understand that the five years after the First World War changed the course of my life entirely. My youth was spent on the land, on a barren smallholding, in a cottage of one, earthen, floor; and then I became a townsman, my feet on paving stones, and the walls of streets pressing in on me. On the way from Llwynpiod to Llwynpia, from Rhydypandy to Tonypandy, I stepped out of yesterday and into today. But where exactly I hit upon that road, I cannot for certain tell . . . (p. 21)

Chapter II

IT MAY NOT BE FAR FROM ABERYSTWYTH TO THE RHONDDA FAWR, BUT IT was a long way for Kitchener Davies from 'Welsh' Wales to Alfred Zimmern's 'American Wales'; from a culture respectful of T. Gwynn Jones's *Ymadawiad Arthur* to one dominated by Arthur J. Cook and Arthur Horner. He arrived to live with Bodo Mari, and to teach at Blaengwynfi primary school, in 1926 – the now legendary year of the nine-day General Strike and the heroically futile seven-month stop-out of the miners. This turned out to be the Waterloo of the visionary *Marxisant* militants in the unions but served only to strengthen the Rhondda proletariat's long-term commitment to the more moderate and pragmatic socialist politics of the Labour Party. In spite of Kitchener's best efforts, Labour was to win 112 out of the 118 coalfield contests for Westminster seats between 1918 and 1939, with the two Rhondda constituencies, where almost 75 per cent of male voters were miners, proving particularly impregnable.

At the time of Kitchener's arrival, the peoples of the Rhondda were about to be broken on the wheels of the very pits that had brought them together from far and wide. Soon, almost half a million would migrate to England, seeking not only work but escape from the grimmest social deprivation. The statistics tell their own story: output dropping from 33 per cent of world production to 3 per cent; male unemployment obstinately standing at 60.8 per cent by 1934; 46 per cent of the children officially declared to be undernourished in 1935. And still the successive London governments did next to nothing, despite being urged by distinguished economists such as J. M. Keynes and Hilary Marquand to institute a programme of economic regeneration.

Statistics were also Kitchener's way of getting to grips with the enormity of the situation: 14 per cent of dairies and 12 per cent of greengrocers closed, 18.9 per cent of children undernourished, 70 per cent unemployment, 6.3 per cent migration, he noted in 1928, proceeding to analyse the intolerable pressure on families (eight people surviving on 30 shillings, thirteen of which went on rent), and on councils whose basic, subsistence-level services themselves depended on the rates paid by workers now degradingly reduced to slum dwellers. His analysis appeared in *Yr Efrydydd*, the journal of Urdd y Deyrnas, a Christian ecumenical movement in which Kitchener had become very active. He shared the Urdd's passionate concern for international peace, and saw conditions in the Rhondda as deriving from a nexus of causes, including the Versailles Treaty's punitive treatment of the German Ruhr (*From Reparation to Industrial Ruin* was the subject of his friend, George M. Ll. Davies's famous pamphlet) and the inherent belligerence both of communism and of the international capitalism that sponsored imperialism.

In 1934–5 the League of Nations Union (a special Welsh branch of which had been formed by Lord Davies of Llandinam) arranged a Peace Vote in which 62 per cent of Welsh voters supported disarmament. Ever since the First World War, there had been a strong broad-front movement in Wales in favour of international peace. That such movements could consist of a motley and cantankerous group of individuals – leonine communists reluctant to lie down with SCM [Student Christian Movement] sheep – was Kitchener Davies's acerbic conclusion in a report filed for *Yr Efrydydd* in 1933 on the National Peace Council conference he had attended in Oxford. Secretly, he felt that he, too, could support a 'just' war waged by the oppressed in Bombay, but judged it unwise to voice that opinion at an Oxford conference where the threatening presence of the British fleet off the west coast of India seemed plainly unobjectionable. And he was incandescent at the smug middle-class suggestion that schools might educate a generation of pacifists – when hopelessness, relieved only by whispers of bloody insurrection, stared Rhondda school-leavers in the face.

In a report he filed from Geneva in 1933 on the World Disarmament Conference, a grasp of *realpolitik* is apparent in his scrupulously detailed analysis of the difficulties that had led to the conference's suspension. His account of the Urdd's 1934 conference at Chester featured approving summaries of the many lectures on the iniquities of the market economy. A new economic order respecting fundamental human needs (emotional, spiritual, psychological) and regulated by a spirit of mutuality, co-operation and social inclusiveness – this, Kitchener agreed, was the blueprint for a Christian community and a genuinely democratic society. Statism, whether capitalist, socialist, communist or fascist, had been rendered obsolete by science and technology; the future would see a return to small-scale communities, familial in character.

These ideals were consonant with the ideology of Plaid Cymru, the Welsh Nationalist Party Kitchener joined shortly after its foundation in 1925, and which he served with self-consuming energy to the end of his life. The example of Ireland, the extinguishing of the last glimmer of Liberal sympathy for the old Home Rule ideals of Cymru Fydd, and the rise of a British Centralist Labour party – these account not only for the formation of Plaid Cymru but for the significant support it soon attracted from the likes of the Welsh writers, ministers and intellectuals who became its natural leaders. Kitchener was a devotee of the Summer Schools, the annual jamborees used so effectively by the party to create camaraderie, raise morale, educate opinion and open up new horizons. But at the end of the 1932 school, held in Brynmawr in honour of the Quaker settlement for the unemployed, he found himself regretting the absence of 'manual workers and of business men', and feeling Plaid was beginning to suffer from the old Welsh weakness – 'it talks too much' (*Welsh Nationalist* I, 9, p. 6). Together with the distinguished writer Kate Roberts and her husband, Morris Williams, he set about making the party more streetwise and case-hardened in what the English middle class were calling 'Tonypandemonium' following the riots of 1910 and the town's notoriety as the place where *The Miners' Next Step* had been published in 1912.[3]

Preaching the noble cause inevitably took on a shrill note when it came down to soap-boxes on street-corners and a voice raised to drown out traffic and the obstreperous wags. But Kitchener excelled at the vulgate of the street, and on Tonypandy square he became the Tommy Farr of verbal pugilists, indestructible in his inevitable defeat by the Joe Louis of Labour. He and his friends also played their part in establishing *The Welsh Nation*, the English-language organ Plaid somewhat reluctantly launched to recruit English speakers. The April 1933 issue carried his blistering piece challenging 'paralysed Nationalists' to abandon prim respectability, to canvass door to door, to pit wits against questioners and to test their political philosophy against hecklers. Kitchener himself underwent this trial by fire in the Rhondda and farther afield throughout the twenty years of his campaigning for District and Parliamentary seats (as a teacher, he was prevented from contesting a County seat). Everywhere, he was up against the formidable new machine politics of a proletarian society, involving Lodge officials, organic intellectuals, Labour MPs, and new ward bosses whose minds seemed to opponents to be 'no wider than a seam of coal.'[4]

After Kitchener's death, his exploits became magnified into legend in the affectionate memories of his party's colleagues. Kate Roberts remembered cider, bread and cheese for supper in Kenry Street at the end of an exhausting day's canvassing, with natives of Tregaron and Dyffryn Nantlle dazedly asking each other what on earth they were doing in the Rhondda. Wynne Samuel recalled his quip when a brick aimed at him by a heckler missed its target and struck his friend: 'Look, there's a man not afraid to shed his blood for Wales!' (p. 6). Although he hated communism, he liked communists such as Harry Pollitt and enjoyed sharing a soap-box with him, each taking it in turn to act as barker and warm-up man for the other's main act. For him, the slur in the description of Maerdy as 'Little Moscow' was not in the 'Moscow' but in the diminutive 'little' so readily applied by England to all things Welsh. Zestfully humorous, and a natural connoisseur of street theatre, he cherished as a music-hall turn the moment when a speaker, exasperated with his apathetic audience, disgustedly exclaimed 'Comrades, you do dant me, you do look so bloody dull!' But although Kitchener himself was renowned for his good-natured repartee, he claimed to recall only one occasion when his tongue had untied itself in time. After three senior members of Plaid Cymru, Saunders Lewis, Lewis Valentine and D. J. Williams, had set fire to Penyberth in 1936, Kitchener entered the staff-room in Pentre Grammar School to the gibe that they must have used 'England's Glory' matches; 'no, they were Pioneer' was his instant reply ('Adfyw', p. 23).

'Humour', wrote the Porth writer Gwyn Thomas with Rhondda wit in mind, 'is a nervous condition. Listen to laughter. It has a strange sinister sound; the yelping of an uneasy pack.'[5] For a sensitive outsider, facing the Rhondda of the thirties could be a disconcerting experience, as Saunders Lewis, the charismatic leader of Plaid Cymru, discovered in 1932. Driving through the blighted valleys, he experienced a panic attack, and took refuge with friends: 'I did not tell them that it was the frightening, unnerving experience of that drive, and the realisation of the insane horror of the elongated bedlam of the industrial valley that made me turn in to them to keep my mind clear.'[6] That Bosch-like vision of the apocalyptic collapse of (Welsh) civilization into anarchy found disturbing expression in his poem 'The Deluge, 1939'. It also made him declare 'My Country the Worst Hell in Europe Today', adding prophetically 'that what the political future held for Wales was a choice between Communism and Christian Nationalism.'

This was also the theme of Kitchener's seminal essay in 1937 for the new progressive periodical, *Heddiw*. Capitalism and socialism/communism were Siamese twins, he declared, joined by their common hostility to private property, although the aim of the one was monopoly and the other a despotic state. Both saw themselves in Calvinist terms as the predestined elect of the divine law of Progress and Development. Both were secular religions devoted to the gospel of materialism. Both worshipped the machine and its new religion of mass production. Both ruthlessly policed their subject societies to eliminate all individualism and cultural difference. The only alternative to such dystopias was a Christian nationalism whose regard for the spiritual worth of each individual was underwritten by a respect for private property, and whose recognition of the value of community found expression in its policy of economic co-operation.

'Government by *anonymity* not by *democracy*' was the characteristic of a statist political order staffed by a faceless clerkocracy; that was the message hammered home by Kitchener in 'Senedd y Llan', a series of articles for Plaid's paper, *Y Ddraig Goch*. 'Senedd y Llan'; literally 'The Church Parliament', the Welsh phrase is redolent of a nostalgia for the intimate community politics of an arcadian village. There was also the hint of a nostalgia of an even more disarmingly antique kind. In a contemporaneous article, Kitchener's friend, George M. Ll. Davies, a genteel but gentle-souled Christian activist, wrote of a sea of despair dotted only with islands of hope, such as the Maes-yr-haf social settlement in Trealaw with which he was closely associated. These were the modern equivalent, he suggested, of ancient spiritual refuges such as Bardsey Island and the 'Llan' of the early Celtic saints.[7]

Davies's intense commitment to a Social Gospel was shared by a Kitchener who used to point, like a good carpenter's son, to the crossbeams in house construction as evidence of the practical role of Christianity. In 'Arwydd y Grog', a virtuoso Welsh essay of the early thirties, later recycled in English, he displayed an encyclopaedic interest in the sign of the cross from the time of the Assyrians and Egyptians to the modern Union Jack. This extraordinary compilation of legend, history and anthropology includes materials Kitchener could exploit in three different ways; for political purposes (the Nazi cross had anciently signified bounty in India, China and Japan), for religious instruction (Kitchener was an energetic lay-preacher), and for creative writing (his ability to use symbols as unique means of emotional and experiential exploration became powerfully evident later in *Meini Gwagedd* and *Sŵn y Gwynt sy'n Chwythu*).

Capitalism excelled, of course, at using the blandishment of symbols for creative branding of products. Drooling over the seductive promise of Golden Dawn, Rose Dew and Snowdrift for ninepence in the local cafés and soda fountains, Kitchener, only half ironically, suggested rural Wales might benefit economically from rebranding its milk, butter and cheese for a new consumer market. Writing in Welsh about 'Enwau Soniarus a Dieithr' (mellifluous and strange names), he was able to make wonderful new verbal confections out of these Bracchi products that give him a new taste for language as well as offering a new language of taste. An introduction of the 'old language' to brash new Rhondda was, in any case, overdue. Sour comments such as those of Kate Roberts, that Welsh-medium education alone could save the Rhondda from pagan materialism, served only to confirm the working class in its opinon that Welsh-speakers considered themselves a cut above and were a class apart.[8]

To teach Welsh in the Rhondda of the Depression was to belong to 'the suicide squad', the hapless trio that included scripture and music teachers. Already seen as backward, parochial and socially divisive, Welsh was now conclusively labelled useless; between 1931 and 1951 the number of Welsh-speakers in the Rhondda dwindled from 45.4 per cent to 29 per cent. A number of enlightened policy decisions taken by the education authority under the leadership of the director of education, R. R. Williams, were frustrated at the chalk face by apathy and hostility as well as by genuine practical difficulties. At secondary level, where Kitchener ended up teaching, he resorted to chanting the names of central European rivers in a humorous attempt to persuade the children he could speak genuinely useful foreign languages. Outside school, he tried to reinforce the residual Welsh-language culture of the valleys by involving himself in a spectrum of cultural activities, including extension classes on the work of writers such as Ben Bowen, the doomed young poet who had spent his brief life in the turn-of-the-century Rhondda where Welsh-speakers had still been in a majority.

The Pandy Players (Cwmni Drama'r Pandy), who performed Cwm Glo in 1935. Among the cast are the author, centre front; to his right, his sister, Tish Harcombe; to his left, Kate Roberts; centre back, his future wife, Mair Rees; to her left, Morris Williams, Kate's husband.

Ben Bowen's achievements were honoured at the 1928 National Eisteddfod in Treorci. There the Mr Magoo character of the Welsh-language sanhedrin first became grotesquely apparent as they blithely ignored a London magistrate's insulting remark that Welsh girls in service were arrant thieves. They then struck up 'Cwm Rhondda' to drown out the communist hecklers when Prime Minister Stanley Baldwin, one of the architects of the Rhondda's ruin, rose to address the massed faithful in the big pavilion. It was therefore in character when one of the Eisteddfod's major prizes was awarded to a saccharine poetic portrait of 'Shoni', the brave, cultured, generous, noble-spirited Welsh collier. Some four years later, a Kitchener turned angry young man by such humbug outraged the Welsh public by substituting a big pinch of salt for the sugar customarily used in the recipe for cooking the books whenever the Welsh 'gwerinwr' (whether farmer or collier) was described in print. He then proceeded to stir the mix very thoroughly, by touring his own production of his controversial play.

So notorious did *Cwm Glo* become that a whiff of the scandal reached even the London dailies. A leering, lascivious, dissolute and depraved Welsh miner, with a trollop of a daughter who ends up turning Cardiff whore – just the ticket for an English press both contemptuous of Welsh puritanism and eager to blame the condition of the Rhondda on the miners themselves. The play's actual message was, though, the exact opposite. Balancing 'chapel' miner against 'greyhound' miner, downtrodden Welsh 'Mam' against pert Welsh hoyden, morally bewildered worker against morally corrupt manager, Kitchener was explicitly saying these people were not merely living in Cwm Glo (Coal Vale), they were all formed, or rather deformed, by the malign capitalist values permeating every aspect of life there, frustrating natural desire and strangling personal relations. What is prostitution, asks Kitchener (perhaps recalling Shaw's *Mrs Warren's Profession*), but a naked admission of the 'spirit' of exploitation at work throughout Cwm Glo? What are gambling and blackmail (Dai Dafis's handy little earners) but admirably lucrative examples of private enterprise? Since the immorality endemic to industrial capitalism is systemic in Cwm Glo, it cannot be entirely escaped by anyone, including the devout. In a central scene, this point is made by the pious old miner, Dic Evans, who tries to offer, through the Biblical parable of God's concern for the least sparrow that falls, a vision of loving mutuality starkly different from the prevailing ethos. Like John Price in J. O. Francis's seminal coalfield drama, *Change* (1912), Dic Evans represents an earlier, Mabonite era of industrial good will.

But it is the despair of the very different Rhondda of the Depression years that is darkly inscribed in the very structure of Kitchener's play, as the last act constitutes a kind of parodic inversion of so much (including Dic's hopeful 'sermon') that has gone before. Just as Dai has now become the effective 'manager' of the actual Manager who had dismissed him, so he holds up a mocking mirror of themselves to virtually all of the play's leading characters, showing the hypocrisy of the respectable and the naive ineffectuality of the good. Indeed, the sombre vision that is at the heart of *Cwm Glo* is most evident in the irony of the relationship between the 'good' and the 'bad' miner. Dic Evans the Christian had tried to save even depraved Dai from the sack, but was himself eventually forced into retirement; so when Dai, through blackmail, later gained power over the mine's Manager, he 'repaid' Dic's kindness by putting him back in work. However, this was not Vice's tribute to Virtue, but rather a vengefully parodic mockery of a good deed. The real power of *Cwm Glo* lies in such disturbing moral distortions rather than in the unconvincing resolution provided in its melodramatic ending, with Dai's daughter heading for Cardiff's 'traffic' (a nice example of the play's subversions of euphemism) while Dai himself is killed off when he is knocked to the ground by the man he has been blackmailing, leaving the curtain to fall on Dic piously reciting the Lord's Prayer. That ending was in effect rejected by Kitchener himself, shortly before his death, when he agreed (presumably) to the BBC Welsh Region's broadcasting of an edited and abridged version of the play, minus its original grand finale.

'Our aims and our programme are every whit as revolutionary as those of Communism,' wrote Saunders Lewis of Plaid Cymru in 'My Country the Worst Hell in Europe Today' (1932), and *Cwm Glo* is a revolutionary work in both theatrical and political terms. The Plaid Cymru connection, albeit crudely understood, helped damn the play in the eyes of some of its most vociferous critics, who nevertheless preferred to echo the moral objections levelled against the work from its inception. A fine piece of theatre, but too morally offensive to be staged, had been the adjudicators' verdict at the Neath National Eisteddfod (1934) on *Cwm Glo*, a revised version of the play *Adar y To* (Sparrows) which Kitchener had entered in the 1932 National Eisteddfod at Port Talbot. Nevertheless, the poet Cynan, Nonconformist minister, the 'Donald Wolfit of Wales', and newly appointed official government censor of Welsh drama, duly licensed the play for performance – was it a coincidence, one wonders, that his work had been flatteringly quoted in the text?

After the senate of the University College of North Wales, Bangor, refused permission to the students' Drama Society to perform *Cwm Glo*, a pioneering production was toured by the highly respected Swansea Welsh Drama Company. ('Oh you nation of vipers' was Kitchener's reaction to the news that one of the eisteddfod adjudicators was associated with the company.) 'Common', 'Filthy', 'Putrid', Ghastly', 'Appallingly disgusting' were some of the comments heard in the Amman valley where, as the *News Chronicle* noted, sections of the audience claimed the play cast 'vulgar and uneducated reflections on the mining community'. Hollywood 'pictures' were blamed in part for the sensationalist, sexually suggestive character of a work by an author whose bestial imagination was likened to that of the great *bête noire*, Caradoc Evans. Hostile reviewers sniffily attributed the play's huge box-office success to provocative notices in the London morning dailies predicting outcry and public mayhem wherever *Cwm Glo* was performed. The most influential of the play's implacable opponents was Amanwy (David Griffiths), a venerable miner-poet with impeccable Labour credentials (his brother was to become the first Secretary of State for Wales). The very epitome of the famously cultured industrial *gwerin*, and therefore an iconic figure of Welsh-language culture, Amanwy was self-appointed spokesman for the respectable working class, in whose name he roundly condemned Kitchener for prostituting his undoubted talents by libelling the miners of south Wales. Underlying Amanwy's remarks were deep, class-based resentments at the cocky attitudes of this jumped-up, college-educated dramatist, a rabidly anti-Labour member of 'fascist' Plaid Cymru who, or so a newspaper reported, had woundingly characterized Welsh miners as culturally rootless. It is therefore very much to Amanwy's credit that, on another occasion, he could generously congratulate the author of *Cwm Glo* on his ground-breaking achievement and could acknowledge that the theme of the play had seared Kitchener's imagination.

There were others, of course, who rallied to Kitchener's defence, in particular the young Anglo-Welsh artist and writer Ken

Etheridge who had painted the back-cloth for the controversial Ammanford production. Relishing the short shrift given in the play to 'old religious humbug', Etheridge saw Kitchener as a Welsh D. H. Lawrence, 'a man in furious rebellion against the degradation' of mining villages. 'We see the lives of the people . . . going to waste', Etheridge observed angrily, 'and the dirt of their environments is bitten so deeply into their souls that they seem beyond redemption. Who will consider this and call *Cwm Glo* an immoral play? It is the fiercest criticism of industrial life that has yet appeared in dramatic form.' When the text of the play was published, the reviewer for *Heddiw* discovered in it a frankness about sex previously found only in Saunders Lewis's daring novel, *Monica*, and an awareness similar to that in Liam O'Flaherty's *The Informer* of how people could be psychologically crippled by their environment. The review in *Yr Efrydydd*, however, was much more uneasy in tone. Yes, *Cwm Glo* was to be admired for its alertness to the destructive influence of Darwinism, Marxism, Freudianism and various other new determinist ideologies that weakened the sense of personal responsibility, but the play was limitingly fixated on the evil in human nature. The reviewer therefore seconded the opinion of an anonymous author who had warned that 'This vogue of frankness is with many a conscious pose and thus becomes a new form of hypocrisy.'[9]

In the Amman Valley performances by the Swansea company, Clydach Thomas, a wily old ham, had been praised by hostile reviewers for softening the impact of *Cwm Glo* by playing Dai Dafis not as a depraved character but as a waggish rogue. Such wanton misinterpretation may have helped Kitchener decide not only to form a local company of friends (The Pandy Players) and mount his own production but also to take the part of Dai Dafis himself. Pointedly casting his sister, Tish – who was in her thirties at the time – in the part of Dai's 'whorish' young daughter was his typically mischievous answer to the eisteddfod adjudicators' supposedly rhetorical question: was there in Wales a man so lost to decency that he would dare ask his sister to play Marged? In so doing, Kitchener deliberately highlighted two aspects of his play: its sexual boldness (extending even to hints of sexual abuse of daughter by father) and its penetratingly sympathetic understanding of the plight of women in mining communities, an understanding perhaps not wholly unrelated to the author's memories of a mother who had been left to die in childbirth and of a substitute mother who had very probably been seduced by her employer when she was a young girl in service in the valleys. Determined that Tish should not suffer the same fate, Bodo Mari had supervised her strictly, and that pattern of conduct is reproduced in the play when Marged is disastrously spoilt by a mother tragically determined her daughter should not prostitute herself by becoming a husband's slave. It may be no accident that *Cwm Glo* was written just a few years after Kitchener had suffered the third, and last, great hurt of his life: the death of Bodo Mari in 1929.

The play was also written at exactly the same time as 'Y Llysfam' and seems to deal, in concealed form, with the same traumatic issues. By involving Tish and himself in the performing of *Cwm Glo*, Kitchener was in effect confessing that this was indeed a family drama. His identification of himself with the action was very much in keeping with the play's overt message: as one who lived and worked in 'Cwm Glo', he was not apart from the moral squalor, he was a part of it, and admitted as much by having his miners comment sardonically on the perks, privileges and power enjoyed by teachers.

But his work may be personal at a much deeper, psychic level than that. In structure *Cwm Glo* is a revenge play, as is repeatedly made clear in the final act when Dai Dafis and Marged bring all their enemies to book by mounting a kind of play within the play, with Marged ('pretty as vengeance') mimicking their voices and acting their part. As befits people living in a society where personal relations are entangled in the cash nexus, she and her father delight in repaying their enemies in their own coin. And a similarly irresistible desire for revenge is, of course, the driving theme of 'Y Llysfam'. When, therefore, Kitchener decided to play the part of Dai Dafis, he may unconsciously have been recognizing how much of himself was hidden in what one adjudicator had summarily dismissed as 'one of the vilest characters ever created'. Dai's contempt for established authority; his scorn for hypocritical respectability; his nihilistic energy; his sardonic wit and mischief; his twisted passion for exposing the 'truth' – in perverted form, these echo key features of the challengingly 'extremist' character of a Kitchener 'Dafis' who agreed wholeheartedly with Saunders Lewis ('My Country the Worst Hell') that Nationalists needed to be as revolutionary as communists: 'It is no good at all trying to be conciliatory and "reasonable" and moderate. Those are the virtues of office-seekers and timid ineffectuals.'

   No doubt Kitchener was in part irrepressibly defiant by nature – he prided himself on being descended from the wild Georges, a byword for trouble in the Tregaron district. When a stranger once commented on how very many of that family were buried in Tregaron churchyard, a local brusquely replied 'Not half enough of them, the devils.' But as 'Y Llysfam' suggests, Kitchener's furiously renegade energy may also have been strengthened by his earliest experiences. To have his mother 'betray' him by dying when he was six, and to have his father compound that betrayal some twelve years later by selling Y Llain from over his very head, was perhaps to lose all trust early in established, socially respected 'authority'. But if Dai Dafis was in this regard Kitchener's dark alter ego, then Dic Evans (the pious old Christian) was the trusting, believing side of his personality. Kitchener's life and work consisted of a dialogue between them – each keeping the other from decaying respectively into nihilism and into sentimental religiosity. Also intimately important to him as a writer was the difference between the Bible-rich, beautifully idiomatic, but socially anachronistic Welsh spoken by Dic Evans, representative of a passing generation, and the 'debased', 'Anglicized', slovenly and slangy idiolect of Marged, who thereby speaks the language of an entirely different social experience and speech community. How to remake Welsh into a contemporary medium by bringing two such 'languages' as these to bear on each other was the great challenge for the writer.

Personal though the animus behind *Cwm Glo* may have been, no one was more aware than Kitchener Davies that the play belonged to a theatrical tradition already so well established it was in danger of parodying itself. As early as 1935 he was quoted in the press as saying that '*Cwm Glo* deserved neither to be overpraised nor overcriticized; it is nothing but an attempt that was successful in part and a failure in part'.[10] The passion for Ibsen ('the Arch Druid of realism') that seized Welsh dramatists in the opening decades of the century had produced several arresting social issue plays by a generation of young writers, such as W. J. Gruffydd, D. T. Davies and R. G. Berry, keen to dispose of a sclerotic, spiritually bankrupt Nonconformist establishment. Hypocrisy-bashing and deacon-baiting became the norm in plays routinely welcoming society's black sheep back into the fold, while in *Change* J. O. Francis focused attention on the violent clash in the coalfield between the old consensual and conciliatory elements and the militantly confrontational leaders of a new, class-conscious proletariat. Explaining in 1936 that 'the radio wants pioneers', Kitchener expressed his hope that the new medium might attract new experiments from Francis and his kind, whose work in Welsh theatre 'has not yet been surpassed'.

These powerful and influential plays marked the beginning of what became, between the two world wars, a remarkable social phenomenon as Wales was swept by a craze for amateur drama in both Welsh and English. By the mid thirties there were about 500 companies at work, with roughly the same number of plays in circulation. Workmen's halls, welfare halls, chapel vestries, all had their rival outfits, with villages occasionally boasting as many as eight different companies, some of which became stars of local and national competitions. From Dan Matthews's famed group in the west to the Moss Players of Maerdy in the Rhondda Fach, from Botffari in the north to Cwmni'r Gwter Fawr in the Amman valley, the stellar companies commanded a huge popular following, and the Aberdare Theatre Company had a standing membership of 300. But local performers were also well supported as tickets for week-long drama festivals regularly sold within hours of the booking office opening. While productions ranged in standard from the gor-blimey to the highly sophisticated, the movement did produce a corps of accomplished actors some of whom (Meredith Edwards, Clifford Evans, Rachel Thomas) went on to have distinguished careers in theatre, radio and film.

Although Kitchener himself was to translate two English-language plays into Welsh, he shared the misgivings of many intellectuals about the dependence of Welsh-language theatre on light comedies and other West End fare. A genuinely Welsh repertoire was needed not only for the sake of the language and its literature but also because Kitchener followed his model, Saunders Lewis, in believing drama to be, as Yeats, Synge and O'Casey had shown, a key consciousness-raising medium for building a nation. Kitchener was not, however, a politician turned playwright. Totally in thrall to theatre, he clearly saw that Wales had always lacked the complex sociocultural conditions (an urban civilization, a middle class, a commercial theatre, an educated audience, professional personnel) necessary for the development of a strong drama tradition, so talk of a 'Great Welsh Play' was chauvinistic nonsense. 'We Welsh dramatists know how childish is our work,' he declared,[11] enthusiastically involving himself in attempts (such as drama weeks, eisteddfod competitions, discussion forums, theatre workshops) to create an informed, knowledgeable culture, an effective infrastructure and a more co-ordinated programme of activities. Performances of *Cwm Glo* had, he felt, merely set the work of an apprentice dramatist before a theatrically immature audience, with predictable results, and even before the boos and hisses had died away he was already distancing himself from the play's realism.

That Kitchener was a most reluctant realist is evident in all the many lively articles, in Welsh and in English, he contributed to journals and newspapers (including *The News Chronicle*) during the years of his 'notoriety'. He is shooting from the hip – the comments do not add up to a fully coherent, internally consistent, set of theoretical objections – but as such his essays serve only to emphasize the extent of his problems as Welsh-language dramatist and the corresponding urgency and immediacy of his response. Moreover, they indicate his sensitivity not only to the practical constraints of realism but also to the ideologies inscribed in its ostensibly neutral and authoritative conventions.

First adopted as a style for anatomising rural, chapel-centred society, Welsh realism struggles, Kitchener suggests, when called upon to deal with industrial communities, so writers simply dress the familiar old rural types in new industrial clothes ('In art industrial Wales is a derelict rural culture'). There are also insurmountable language problems when representing valleys life, English being not only the language of the governing and middle classes (from managers to shopkeepers to policemen) but also increasingly of the workers. Therefore there can be no possibility of using Welsh convincingly as a 'realistic' language, and in any case, any attempt to do so runs into the additional difficulty of linguistic register, since there is no ready Welsh equivalent of neutral, standard English speech ('the King's English'); speakers of different dialects are mutually incomprehensible to each other; what passes for Rhondda Welsh is nothing but a thin, Anglicized *patois*; and to use dialect is to inhibit Wales's ability to experience itself not, in colonial terms, as a collection of tribal regions but as a single post-colonial nation. Similarly, since the realist mode is the idiom of the modern, it serves to confine Wales to its present, colonial status by denying it access to its alternative, pre-colonial past. Realism purports to represent life in its ordinariness, but since ordinary life is typically banal and undramatic, it has to be silently translated, for stage purposes, into unnaturally heightened terms; hence the paradox that realism degenerates into melodrama and sensationalism.

These are essays speaking eloquently to Kitchener Davies's predicament as a Welsh-language writer, and they include highly prescient passages:

> Once more languages have been mixed in this modern Babel [of south Wales]: the minister is a university graduate replete with Morris-Jones Welsh; the deacon mixes his scripture-texts with Marxist jargon; the impersonal grocer has a Glamorgan accent; the mechanised carpenter refuses to be wholly proletarian for he still owns his Anglesey dialect. Is the Welsh artist more than the Almighty that he can put the unity of artistic form upon this chaos? . . .
> Galsworthy could not wish for a better social conflict. But a Welsh Galsworthy is immediately faced with a particular limitation that diverts his imaginative rumination from the thought-context of his story to the exacting demands of form.
> [The two languages of modern Wales] stand for distinctive and different national life-values. Perhaps the long-awaited masterpiece of art in Wales will be bilingual since Welsh life is a thin layer between two thick slices of English – a little good meat sandwiched between the slave mentality of quasi-polite possessors on the one side and the slave mentality of the disinherited on the other. No artist will succeed without taking the content of the Welsh element and the content of the English element into account; to neglect the one or the other is to guarantee a misrepresentation of life which is of necessity an artistic lie.[12]

Kitchener also had one other, fundamental reservation about realist writing. For him, realism was, paradoxically, an artificial artistic convention powerless to access the deepest realities of human experience, since they exist at deep emotional and psychological levels that prosaic realism lacks the language to explore. In due course, *Meini Gwagedd* and *Sŵn y Gwynt sy'n Chwythu* were to plumb those very depths, and Kitchener's hunger for an artistic and linguistic medium better suited to 'the outrageous truth the [real] dramatist tells' is apparent in a striking passage in the *News Chronicle* article in which he asked 'Will 1936 Produce the Great Welsh Playwright?' His comments also indicate how aware he was of realism's secret bias towards a secular view of the world:

> The first great Welsh dramatist will be he who ventures on a voyage of discovery into a sea that Welsh artists, possibly because of the objective tradition of our poetry, have not charted. The subjective

psychological play that manifests the twists and tortures, the raptures and exultations, the frustrations and achievements within the human soul, facing the elemental passions of humanity, remains as yet to be written.

To write it, he poignantly noted, required 'concentration' and 'experimental work'. The former he, with his passionate political commitments, often found it difficult to supply; upon the latter, however, he was always restlessly engaged, even providing himself, through the Pandy Players and their successors, with a 'workshop' of sorts for his experimentation.

However, the two experiments in historical writing that followed *Cwm Glo* were, to put it mildly, misconceived. The appropriate way to stage history was of marked interest to the period, and the modes adopted varied as widely as the versions of the Welsh past on offer, ranging from the sophisticated productions of Saunders Lewis to the more popular attempts of Cynan and, of course, the populist historical pageants that were such a feature of the age, following that Hollywood epic, The National Pageant of Wales (1909), featuring 5,000 participants and 30,000 spectators. As the Depression bit, and international tensions grew, so did pageant fever understandably spread, offering (as a reporter noted of the grand Swansea Pageant) the 'colour and exotic glamour of the past, contrasted with the modern age, with its "drab robots of history" '. Hilariously anachronistic in costume and Monty Pythonesque in 'dialogue', these sumptuous instances of *son et lumière* usually peddled a cartoon version of Welsh history suitably tailored to the patriotically British tastes of the loyal participating citizenry. No wonder, therefore, that in 1934 a plea was made for the Eisteddfod to balance the picture. 'It would be a great step forward,' argued John Ellis Williams, 'to get the Welsh nation alive to the facts of its history, and Welsh pageants should not be allowed to die.'[13] And in such history plays Kitchener saw an opportunity to use a 'correct' Welsh without thereby violating the illusion of authenticity.

Unfortunately, what Kitchener provided in his vaguely poeticized one-act play, *Ynys Afallon* (The Isle of Avalon, 1935) was a great step backwards in an attempt, he ominously remarked in *The News Chronicle* ('Will 1936 Produce the Great Welsh Play?'), 'to create the beautiful fairy tale a history tale must of necessity be'. A poor work, as unintentionally comical in places as the pageants it was meant to replace, it is also revealing of the simplistic (and at times disturbing) aspects of Plaid's historiography in that period. Apparently intended as a production to mark the four hundredth anniversary of 1536, *Ynys Afallon* treats most of modern Welsh history as a disaster stemming from the baleful Act of Union. (Once again, betrayal, leading to the loss of inheritance, is the wellspring of the action.) Before the Tudor Act there had been hierarchical order, cultural richness, spiritual exaltation; after it there was (apart from the redeeming influence of an originally 'foreign' Methodism) only the cultural decline and spiritual degradation attendant upon the greedy grasping by the Welsh of the opportunity to gain wealth and status by joining in imperialistic England's military adventures. Meanwhile, the memory of Wales's independent past was best preserved in the rural, upland areas (here Kitchener explicitly acknowledged the symbolic geography of Peate), while the lowlands of south and east were settled by an alien invading culture.

This, then, is the historical fairy tale worked out, in the one-act *Ynys Afallon*, in symbolic terms of the defeat of Arthur at Camlan. Kitchener concentrates on the aftermath; Arthur's retreat to Avalon and the thwarting by Bedivere, who hurls Excalibur into the lake, of attempts made by those who cravenly desert the fallen king (primarily represented in the play by a court poet turned cunning lawyer, opportunistic politician and Lloyd George lookalike) to seize the sword they covet both for its jewelled handle and for the military might it magically bestows. It is a pity that the play reads so badly and would be even worse to act (Rossetti-ish damsels and holy nuns), given that Kitchener had been so powerfully motivated to write it. Since the late twenties, he had been pondering, in letters to his old college teacher, T. Gwynn Jones, how he might write a sequel to the latter's great, epoch-making poem of 1902, *Ymadawiad Arthur*, which had so memorably ended by turning Bedwyr (Bedivere) into a heart-breaking symbol of the modern Welsh artist's lonely individual responsibility to preserve the possibility of cultural renewal (Avalon) by keeping faith with his language and culture, even though the old power and magic (Arthur and Excalibur) had departed from the land: 'Bedwyr yn drist a distaw / at y drin aeth eto draw.' ('Silently and sadly, Bedwyr returned to the distant struggle.')

Dies Irae; the habit of peppering the unfortunate text with Latin tags (*Lachrymae Rerum*, *Dulce et Decorum est*, *Pax Romana*) begins with the title of Kitchener's second historical play. It is AD 61 and the British tribes, under their fierce war-lords Boudicca and Dyfnrig, are about to wreak revenge – that theme again – on Suetonius' Imperial Army of occupation for its brutal ways (rape, cruelty, extortion). However, the best laid plans of war-lords go astray as Boudicca's daughter falls in love with a Roman captive, a young captain about to be sacrificed to the blood-thirsty gods whose 'divine' assistance the Britons are seeking on the eve of battle. We are, then, in all-too-familiar theatrical company in this play, as, over four rather dreary acts, the stage is filled with Secret Paths and Star-Crossed Lovers much given to sentimental effusions, and it unfortunately does not help that Kitchener's heart should nevertheless be in the right place. *Dies Irae* is an anti-war tract that identifies the familiar features of the kind of war fever that had gripped Wales in 1914 and that was, or so Kitchener very much feared, about to do so again in 1936. The rhetoric of propaganda (defending women, children and civilization); the appropriation of religious language (a just war; in God our trust); men's susceptibility to the macho glamour of military trappings and to the cult of bravery; women's scorn for 'cowardice' (the white feather); these and other notorious incentives to war are dutifully exposed in the play. And central to the work is a plea for a true Christian ethic of love and forgiveness to triumph over a barbaric, pseudo-Christian, state culture of revenge. But *Dies Irae* remains a play over which it would be kind to draw a veil rather than one on which one would want to raise the curtain.

Both *Ynys Afallon* and *Dies Irae* are products of a period when Kitchener Davies was becoming increasingly anxious and angry about 'Wales's place in England's [military] conspiracies', as he entitled the piece he published in *Heddiw* in 1936. Recalling that Wales had originally been annexed in 1536 because England wanted to make sure 'its back door was shut', Kitchener argued that the same thinking (animated in part by fear of the unemployed proletariat) still guided government policy. To tie Wales securely to England, factory sites were being developed from Oxford to the Severn, Welsh workers were being encouraged to migrate there, a Severn bridge would be built for business and military traffic, and derelict south Wales would be converted into 'a colonial dumping ground' for factory products. To protect the vulnerable Welsh coast safe from possible invasion by Irish or European enemies, military bases were already being established in the Vale of Glamorgan, Pembrey and Pembrokeshire in the south, and in Porth Neigwl (The Devil's Kitchen) in the north. Meanwhile civil servants in Whitehall were no doubt preparing for possible air attack by drawing up plans to move the nerve-centre of government either to Edinburgh or to Cardiff.

Kitchener Davies was, of course writing his essay in the light of developments at Penyberth in the Llŷn peninsula, where the government, ignoring Wales-wide, cross-party protests, was pressing ahead with plans to pull down a historic old farmhouse, with strong cultural associations, in order to build an RAF bombing school. In September 1936, three of Plaid Cymru's most respected leaders, including Saunders Lewis, set fire to the site and then gave themselves up for trial by 'English' law. It was an event that was to leave as deep a mark on Wales as had the 1926 strike.

Chapter III

While awaiting the Old Bailey trial that would send him to Wormwood Scrubs, Saunders Lewis wrote a remarkable radio play, *Buchedd Garmon* (The Life of Germanus), for broadcasting on the BBC Welsh Region Service. Innovative in its use of a free verse form fashioned out of traditional Welsh metres (radio might, Lewis suggested, be the best modern medium for verse drama), *Buchedd Garmon* also riveted listeners' attention by creating an unexpected parable for the plight of Wales in the 1930s out of the fifth century theological struggle between the Briton, Pelagius (in whose heretical doctrine of human free will Lewis saw the disastrous seeds of modern secular and religious individualism) and the bishop of Auxerre, Germanus (advocate of the orthodox belief in the innate sinfulness of the individual and the resulting need to belong to the saving Christian collective of the Catholic Church). One famous passage in particular was to resonate in the imagination of 'Jim bach y Llain' as a desolating yet challenging image of cultural disinheritance:

> A vineyard entrusted to my care is Wales, my country,
> to transmit to my children,
> and to my children's children,
> an eternal inheritance.
> And see, the swine rush upon her to foul and defile her.
> I, this present, call on my friends,
> Everyman and scholar,
> come join me in the gap,
> stand with me in the pass,
> so that may be saved for the generations to come the
>   purity that used to be.[14]

Both *Meini Gwagedd* and *Sŵn y Gwynt sy'n Chwythu* would, in a way, be deeply personal meditations on the implications of this passage.

Keen as ever to de-Anglicize and to Europeanize Wales, Lewis carefully refrained from acknowledging the longstanding interest of English dramatists – from Phillips, Bottomley and Flecker to Auden, MacNeice, Charles Williams and Dorothy L. Sayers – in sponsoring the return of poetry to the modern theatre. Yet of direct and unquestionable relevance to Lewis and to Kitchener was the greatest of these poet dramatists, T. S. Eliot, whose *Murder in the Cathedral* (1935) and *The Family Reunion* (1939) were both testimony to his belief that 'verse-drama and non-realistic presentation' were alone suitable for exploring the religious dimensions of human experience, because they 'lived in two worlds and dealt naturally with the interaction of those worlds by ritual, emblematic colours and elevated language'.[15] Indeed, there are sections of *The Family Reunion*, a play with which Kitchener became fascinated, where the poetry seems to act like an eerie sonar detector, identifying those deeply subliminal areas of Kitchener's psyche from which his two greatest works would eventually come:

> In an old house there is always listening and more is heard than is spoken.
> And what is spoken remains in the room, waiting for the future to hear it.
> And whatever happens began in the past, and presses hard on the future.
> The agony in the curtained bedroom, whether of birth or of dying,
> Gathers in to itself all the voices of the past, and projects them into the future. (p. 100)

With his one-act play, *Susanna* (1937), however, Kitchener resumed his experimentation with different forms of drama, in this case turning to the Apocrypha and the Bible for the familiar story of the ogling religious elders' attempts to blackmail a virtuous young beauty into satisfying their lust. His (insipidly decorous) treatment of the episode was in keeping with his earlier observation that Welsh dramatists might find in the Bible a usable 'common language' – that is a recognizably 'standard' Welsh and a familiar frame of reference. In his newspaper column headed 'Footlights on the Celtic Stage', he noted that 'the Bible is the only standard literature universally heard and read, and it has already familiarized the Welsh ear to a non-dialect speech and form that in its setting escapes pedantry.' In addition, *Susanna* reflects Kitchener's fundamental need (evident in all his work, from *Cwm Glo* to *Sŵn y Gwynt sy'n Chwythu*) to understand the decline of Wales (and the civilization of the West) in Christian, Biblical terms; and also to attribute that decline to the decay of the authentic spiritual experience of early Calvinist Methodism into secular humanism and religious liberalism. Of course, this was a familiar complaint of Welsh intellectuals of the period, and Kitchener's elders are in effect only a version of the hypocritical deacons that were a staple of Welsh drama. But aware though he was of such a cliché, Kitchener may have been prompted to repeat it for several pressingly personal reasons; first, he may (as *Sŵn y Gwynt sy'n Chwythu* was later to suggest) have harboured an obscure sense of his own life as one of involuntary concealments, subterfuges and performances; secondly, there is his customary intense identification with abused women (also a stock image of suffering Wales); and thirdly, in Susanna's stubborn determination to challenge respected authority, armed only with moral power, he may have sensed a parallel to both his own defiant campaigning against the political odds and the angry resistance of the Rhondda proletariat to the peeping toms of the Means Test (1935). Outmanoeuvring the law was likewise the theme of *Y Tri Dyn Dierth* (1937), a fine translation of *The Three Wayfarers*, Hardy's stage adaptation of one of his *Wessex Tales*. It is a Twm Siôn Catti escapade; an escaped prisoner, a poor man condemned to death for stealing a sheep to feed his starving family, is wily enough to trick the macabre hangman who pursues him into hunting down his brother instead, much to the delight of the good-natured rustics who are drawn into the action. The play was written for an eisteddfod competition (Resolven Social Services Eisteddfod, 1937; Cardiff National Eisteddfod, 1938), like most of the work of an author – intent on mastering what he firmly regarded as a craft – who had written *Cwm Glo* because it was 'a form of literature I wished to understand'.[16] It was, however, what not to do in drama that he primarily learnt by translating Jack Jones's *Land of My Fathers* (*Hen Wlad fy Nhadau*, 1939) at the eisteddfod's request; and his reservations about the play are made apparent in an important discussion he published in *Heddiw* about drama and the National Eisteddfod. He had already outlined his main concern in the *News Chronicle* (13 December 1935): 'One is tempted to ask whether these experiments in realism, which are now a feature of both our radio and stage plays, are not already dated, and whether we should not seek to create a more poetic, mystic or symbolic expression, especially in our native drama.'

But whereas his 1930s newspaper articles had been the working notes of a practitioner, his *Heddiw* essay is the first of several attempts by Kitchener to see his work in relation to a previously hidden tradition of Welsh drama – hidden, as he was tartly to note in a post-war review of Thomas Parry's magisterial *Hanes Llenyddiaeth Gymraeg* (History of Welsh Literature), because drama was invariably omitted even from such otherwise comprehensive surveys. There is therefore a sense in which Kitchener's efforts (complementing similar exploratory essays by D. T. Davies in *The Welsh Outlook*) parallel those of Saunders Lewis in the field of Welsh poetry. Both writers sought to uncover (or to construct) an alternative literary tradition that would facilitate and validate their own creative development.

Kitchener dates the emergence of modern Welsh drama to 1879, when the Eisteddfod, offering a prize for a 'Shakespearean' play in Welsh, initiated a fashion for historical drama, written in a consciously cultured language, that lasted until the advent of the Ibsenist, college-educated dramatists just before the First World War. Being realists, these turned to the vernacular, employing dialectal speech to explore the great changes of their own day: 'This was the period of the death of Nonconformity and the profession of faith, and of the coming of agnosticism and "the new theology"; the period of the death of radicalism and the coming of socialism; the period of the destruction of the rural, cottager-craftsman society, and the creation of the industrial proletariat in the South' (p. 173). And the implications of this change from historical to realist drama found classic expression at the Abergavenny Eisteddfod (1913) in the debate between Elphin, the champion of the new drama, and Llywelyn Williams. Kitchener sides firmly with the latter, seeing realism as declining inexorably into dirty realism, as instanced in his own *Cwm Glo* and in such misguidedly contemporary works as Jack Jones's *Land of My Fathers*. What Kitchener wants is a historical drama (already emergent in J. O. Francis's *Howell of Gwent* and Saunders Lewis's *Buchedd Garmon*), that is genuinely national in outlook, rather than regional or sectional. And he requires of it an elevating poetry capable of bestowing a consequential dignity on characters and events.

Saunders Lewis's then unfinished verse drama, *Blodeuwedd*, was one of the plays praised by Kitchener in his essay, and in *Miss Blodeuwedd*, a play in four 'movements' that remains unpublished, he entered into dialogue with that evident masterwork. In spite of his fiancée's warnings that he is trafficking with spirits and playing god, Alun Prys, a Professor of Celtic Studies, revenges himself on his sceptical academic colleagues by using the magic powers he has learnt in a distant exotic country to free the ancient, legendary Blodeuwedd from her bewitchment, changing her back from an owl into a seductively beautiful young woman. It seems at first that the play is simply offering variants on a familiar theme – the hubristic human lust for knowledge and power, famously instanced in the stories of Dr Faustus and Frankenstein and epitomized by the modern figure of the scientist. But then the emphasis shifts, as Dr Owain Trefor, Prys's friend, falls in love with Blodeuwedd and she with him. By then, Prys has grown afraid of the sexual power and apparent amorality of this unpredictable and uncontrollable female he has created, and he prepares to save Trefor (of whom he is also clearly jealous) from the Lilith-like creature by changing her back again into an owl. Appalled and anguished by such a proposal, Trefor accuses Prys of fearing to face up to the fact that 'his' Blodeuwedd is no mere phantom, or demon, or toy, but a complex human being; flesh and blood, soul and body, good and bad. Nevertheless, the play ends with the lovers thwarted in their attempts to escape to freedom, and in Blodeuwedd being condemned to return again to the dark world whence she came.

At once flippant and intense, and skit, pastiche and tragedy by turns, *Miss Blodeuwedd* is radically unfocused but does touch on several of Kitchener's recurrent, and perhaps obsessive, concerns: the extent of the past's hold over the present, the psychology of revenge, the victimisation of woman by man, the drive to experience life *in extremis*. And there are echoes of Kitchener's own past in Prys's dread of the dark and backward abysm of the unconscious, in Blodeuwedd's shuddering memories of a motherless lamb's inconsolable bleat, and in her shriek out of the night like poor Ann's out of the Tregaron bog. The extent of Kitchener's identification with *Miss Blodeuwedd* is, however, impossible to determine, because the work was jointly authored with Mair Rees, who was shortly to become his wife. That the play comes from the marriage of their two minds is signified by the *nom de plume* on the cover, 'Dafydd Rhys' being an amalgam of their respective surnames. In like fashion, the pair would name their home 'Aeron', after the river connecting Kitchener's Tregaron with Mair's Aberaeron. Indeed, *Miss Blodeuwedd* may be read as a kind of prothalamion, since so much of the discussion and the action relates to love and marriage, from the sly comments on courtship in the first 'movement' to those celebrations of eros in the fourth part that anticipate Kitchener's hymn to sacred passion, 'Nunc Dimittis'.

Having arrived from Cardiganshire to teach in the Rhondda in the early thirties, Mair Rees happened to find lodgings virtually next door to Kitchener. Her interest in the Welsh cultural life of

Bethania Chapel, Llwynypia, 15 April 1940. Standing in the foreground, second from the left is Hannah, Kitchener's stepmother and behind her is Thomas Davies, his father.

Tonypandy led to her joining the Pandy Players, and taking a leading part on stage in *Cwm Glo*. As the relationship between Kitchener and herself developed, he broke off his existing engagement to a lady named Flo Dallimore, an action that caused some pain and acrimony. A native of the valleys, who was not a Welsh-speaker, Flo in one way seems to represent that way of life with which Kitchener was fascinated and yet could never be fully 'at home' – the phrase being ironically appropriate in this connection. In Mair he undoubtedly found a partner whom all his friends and associates regarded as his perfect match, and it may be that the gradual disengagement of his imagination, as a creative writer, from the world of *Y Llysfam* and *Cwm Glo* may reflect that increasing intimacy between himself and Mair that culminated in creative terms in the writing of *Miss Blodeuwedd* and in personal terms in their marriage in 1940 of which three daughters were to be born.

Although Kitchener was several years older than his bride – which makes it noteworthy that *Susanna* is a play about a young wife's loving and passionate fidelity to her elderly husband – their marriage seems to have been an exceptionally contented one. They lived in Aeron, a pleasant detached house, flanked by terraced cottages, on the long Brithweunydd Road leading from Porth to Trealaw, and from there Kitchener travelled up the valley in his Austin Seven to Pentre Secondary School where he had been appointed to teach Welsh in September 1937. Owing to his age, he was exempted from military service (to which he was probably opposed on nationalist grounds) but wartime saw the formation, in nearby Ton Pentre, of a pacifist group of young ministers, writers and intellectuals. Named 'Cylch Cadwgan' (the Cadwgan Circle) after their place of meeting at the home of J. Gwyn Griffiths, in the shadow of Moel Cadwgan, the group had strong European affiliations and a venturesome interest in *avant garde* modernist literature that did not much appeal to a Kitchener who, believing such experimentation to be pretentious, held 'that the only basis for modernity in Welsh literature was Pantycelyn not the Pylon poets'.[17]

There were, nevertheless, points of contact between Aeron and Cadwgan, not least in the person of Rhydwen Williams, an avid Cadwganite who became one of Kitchener's cultural converts and acolytes, and remained in thrall to his magnetic personality, as he admitted in his *Poetry Wales* essay:

> it dawned on me that I was not the same calibre as my friend. I found myself listening to a new political reasoning which was cold and uncompromising. The fireplace of Aeron was of rugged redstone. Kitch would sit on the left side of the hearthstone, warming his hands and flicking his cigarette every other, and it was here in such a posture night after night he would talk . . . We would take a flagon to the small inn next door, fill it, all we could afford, and with a chunk of bread and cheese, I would listen, as listen for dear life I did, as Kitch illumined my dark, inquisitive, dreaming young head.

Kitchener himself was a scathing critic of the sentimentality to which (as the quoted passage indicates) Rhydwen was prone, and once when the young pacifist minister sought comfort after being roughly treated by the 'iron fundamentalists' in his chapel,

Kitchener's terse response revealed his hatred (and fear?) of yielding to weakness and self-pity in the face of life's more brutal challenges: 'Dysga ddiodde', gwboi' ('Learn to suffer, good boy').[18] What particularly impressed Rhydwen was Kitchener's extraordinarily eclectic interest in literature, in ideas, and above all in people. Impatient with his disciple's preciosity, he instanced in all his dealings his genuine egalitarian belief in the talents of Everyman. At Aeron open house was kept for anyone who called, and a motley gang they tended to be. Rhydwen vividly recalled Kitchener's warm tolerance of interruption by people such as Jack Lacey, a man 'physically handicapped, but mentally athletic, who had a dream for the Rhondda'; 'What I was thinkin', see, Kitch, was if we could only just get the capital, see, the initial outlay for the production of zip-fasteners; what I was thinkin', see, Kitch . . .', 'Learn to listen to people like that', was Kitchener's response to Rhydwen's indignant protests at such inconvenient visitations.

From the very outbreak of hostilities, when substantial numbers of English women and children were hastily evacuated to rural areas, the beleaguered Welsh intelligentsia had re-affirmed the central importance of the country village to Welsh culture; and in 1944, this was reflected in the decision to hold the National Eisteddfod in Llandybïe. As one commentator observed at the time: 'To keep alive under the stress of war the Eisteddfod had to return to the sanctuary of the village, and in so doing, it reinvigorated the village itself and the Welsh language and culture with it. It is a lesson for after the war.'[19] A similar lesson was taught to children by Kitchener in the series of playlets entitled *Village Life* ('The Cobbler', 'The Carpenter', 'The Blacksmith') he scripted for Welsh radio's *Awr y Plant* (*Children's Hour*). He took as text those sermons on the virtues of village craftsmen that Iorwerth Peate had written in the guise of sociological studies. And these were, in turn, underpinned by an even weightier text, that Kitchener, in one programme, urged his young listeners to heed: 'All these trust to their hands; and every one is wise in his work. Without these cannot a city be inhabited;

... they will maintain the state of the world, and all their desire is in the work of their craft.'

A very different Biblical text, however, served as epigraph to *Meini Gwagedd* (The Stones of Emptiness), the work Kitchener entered for competition at the Llandybïe 'Village National':

> from generation to generation it shall lie waste; none shall pass through it for ever and ever. But the cormorant and the bittern shall possess it; the owl also and the raven shall dwell in it; and he shall stretch out upon it the line of confusion, and the stones of emptiness . . . And thorns shall come up in her palaces, nettles and brambles in the fortresses thereof; and it shall be an habitation for dragons, and a court for owls.

Some of the deepest anguish in *Meini Gwagedd* derives from the way in which Kitchener uses the language of the Bible against the very society that had so long lived by it; and that turning of language is like the twisting of a knife to disembowel a whole culture. The moral despair and helpless degradation of rural Wales is exposed in a spirit not dissimilar to that in which Patrick Kavanagh was, that very same time, exposing the plight of peasant Ireland:

> No crash,
> No drama.
> That was how his life happened.
> No mad hooves galloping in the sky,
> But the weak, washy way of true tragedy –
> No hope. No lust.
> The hungry fiend
> Screams the apocalypse of clay
> In every corner of this land.[20]

Nothing really happens in *Meini Gwagedd*. Everything is over before the poetry even begins, just as everything was over for the characters before ever their lives began; and all of them are bound together on the wheel of fire of that realization. It is

Michaelmas Eve, and the tormented spirits of the dead revisit the ruins of Glangors-fach, the farm once carved out of the grudging bog but now reclaimed by it. As immediately becomes clear, these ghosts remain shackled to the spot by passions that are still unspent – passions of revenge and resentment, of frustration and smouldering fury. There are two groups, and the focus of attention switches periodically from the one to the other. A father and his two unmarried daughters constitute the threesome who first owned the farm, and theirs is an emotionally incestuous relationship, as they feed off their murderous mutual resentment. The old patriarch curses his daughters for the barrenness that thwarted his intention to hand down the family property to male heirs, and they curse him in return for maiming them emotionally and crippling them sexually through evil possession of their lives. The two brothers and sisters in the other group also give themselves up entirely to mutual recrimination, as each has intimate knowledge of the others' vices; Ifan's brutality to animals, the sexual looseness of Elen and Sal. And the one refrain to which each of the ghosts lends voice, turning the play into an eerie echo-chamber of keening, is that it was the vengeance of the bog that made their lives accursed; that their woe was nursed in that sinister, rocking cradle.

Is it true or false, what they wailingly claim? The unappeasable spirits of *Meini Gwagedd* haunt the mind precisely because the poetry of the text baffles every attempt at a final answer. Yes, they are all morally culpable; but no, there is no certainty that their misdeeds account for all their torment. What are identified as causes at one point resurface as effects at another, and vice versa. Reasons become impossible to tell from rationalisations. Through its echoes and half-echoes, its fearful symmetries of syntax, its desolate refrains, its fateful parallelisms, its phrases as treacherously enticing as bog cotton, the poetry creates a phantasmic world full of restless shape-shifting. Mesmerized by the text, readers leave behind the daylight world of moral clarity and enter the twilight of the double vision. The poetry is integral to the 'action', not least because *Meini Gwagedd* is in profound part *about* language. In an obvious sense, there are too many words in the work; too much is said, and too little done, for too long, to make *Meini Gwagedd* readily 'performable' – a fact recognized by Dafydd Gruffydd when he edited it drastically for a radio broadcast in 1946. Such editing both greatly enhanced the work's performability, and also in a way missed its point and reduced its power. Because Kitchener Davies's point is much the same as Samuel Beckett's; that people talk, desperately and incessantly, precisely because there is nothing to say, nothing to 'do'. With their every word they repeat themselves. Every phrase is a redundant expression. Yet, like Coleridge's Ancient Mariner, no sooner do they stop than they are compelled to start again, from the very beginning. Which is, however, *not* the real beginning – not the root of the thing at all. *Meini Gwagedd* is in part about the inability to get at the root of things – to explain why things at Glangors-fach were as they were – and so what the characters create through the poetry is not a smokescreen of words but a miasma of language that sickens the analytical intelligence. And there are images in the work where its profoundest meanings find powerful symbolic expression. One is that of the Biblical Rachel who cried for her children and would not be comforted, because they were not. (And could not a child dumbly cry for its lost mother in the very same way?) This is the cry that, paradoxically, persists in coming precisely because there is no point in crying. The other is the cry that rises to Rhys's lips, 'the screech escaping from a place more ancient than reason' – the cry that is beyond reason because it is without reason; no necessary and sufficient source for it can ever be identified.

Why should Kitchener write a work so harrowing that Jacob Davies, one of the actors who took part in the first production at Lampeter, was afflicted with depression? It may be that it corresponds to his intuition (not to become full admission until *Sŵn y Gwynt sy'n Chwythu*) that the root of his own personality is also shrouded in inalienable mystery; that he is at bottom a stranger to the whys and wherefores of his own nature; that to try to back-track to source would simply be, as the poet Edward

Thomas movingly said of such an attempt, to find 'an avenue, dark, nameless, without end'[21]; and that creative writing is a futile attempt to find a name for the nameless, and thus to bring self-alienation to an end. There seems to be a suggestive parallel here with 'Y Llysfam', where on his death-bed Glyn wrestles unavailingly with his demons, unable to decide whether, when that motor-bike careered over the edge, he was driving it or it was driving him.

Another work may also be suggestively twinned with *Meini Gwagedd*. At Christmas, 1944, Welsh *Children's Hour* broadcast Kitchener's little play, *Gloria in Excelsis*. It is no more than a seasonal fairy tale. A young man falls in love with a mermaid, attracted to the shore by the sound of Christmas Mass. The lovers marry, thus defying the wrath of her father, king of the ocean's monstrous underwater world, and she duly bears him a son. She is forced to abandon her family, however, when her child stumbles upon the precious crown she has unwisely stolen, at her greedy husband's urgings, from her father's kingdom. The crown empowers the monsters of the deep to reclaim her. But the tale ends happily because, years later, the music of the mass again beckons the mermaid ashore, thus enabling her to break free of her pagan father's savage spell. The play ends with the son's cry of delight at being reunited with his mother: 'Mam! Mam!' Could this not be the wished for 'answer' to Ann's unconscionable shriek and sorrowing Rachel's cry? It is tempting to hear, at the end of *Gloria in Excelsis*, an echo, at least, of that unconscious wish that may have lurked so painfully at the root of Kitchener's being: the wish for the return of his mother. And it is interesting to note that religion is here closely associated with the power to heal by effecting a kind of 'redemption'.

The unresolved, and unresolvable, ambiguities of *Meini Gwagedd* extend even to its form, as if the work had called itself into existence on its own disquieting terms. Is it a poetic drama or a dramatic poem? Kitchener had probably keenly wanted it to be the former, since in an adjudication at the previous year's National Eisteddfod at Bangor he had insisted that 'the poet's imagination is the essence of every authentic drama', and had approvingly quoted an English critic's comment on what poetry had allowed Ibsen to do: 'He achieves in two hours a greater concentration of psychological acumen' than others could achieve in ten years (p. 178). But Kitchener himself may have been uncertain about *Meini Gwagedd* at heart, because he took the unprecedented and disconcerting step of entering it for both a poetry and a drama competition at the Eisteddfod. The response of the two adjudicators proved to be very different. While noting that aspects of the work were better suited to a dramatic reading than to a stage drama, D. Matthew Williams nevertheless regarded it as a remarkable, innovative play that might be made to work successfully in performance. So impressed was he that he urged the Eisteddfod to take the unprecedented step of including the text in the *Cyfansoddiadau* (the annual anthology of prizewinning entries). In contrast, Saunders Lewis, judging the free-verse poetry competition, recognized the poetic power *in potentia* of *Meini Gwagedd* but regarded the work as needing severe editing and reorganization. It was a judgement he was to regret, and to revise, in the light of Prosser Rhys's impassioned advocacy for the poetry in *Y Faner*. And with characteristic intellectual honesty and generosity, Lewis then wrote Kitchener a private letter of apology, explaining that he had been over-hasty in his reading, and adding that if 'the critics and the public learn [from Lewis's example] how fallible a critic can be, and how stupid, then nothing but good can come of that'.

To ask whether *Meini Gwagedd* is play or poem would no longer seem relevant, given our present-day scepticism about fixed genres, but it is likely that the work may be effectively realized in public performance only by creating, as Yeats did for *Purgatory* (a play resembling *Meini Gwagedd*), 'an unpopular theatre and an audience like a secret society where admission is by favour and never to many'.[22] That is, in effect, exactly what was done when *Meini Gwagedd* was staged in Lampeter in 1945 – an experiment all the bolder when it is remembered that the play had been quite closely modelled on the lives of an actual Tregaron family, whose relatives were in the Lampeter audience.

The production was in response to Kitchener's wishes, as reported in the Welsh press. In a letter, he had explained that *Meini Gwagedd* had been written to show that poetry was even more suitable, and necessary, a medium for dealing with contemporary experience than for exploring the historical past. The stage needed to be rid of the melodrama and sentimentality that sullied realism, and had he his time again he would rewrite *Cwm Glo* in poetry, poetry being 'the "antidote" to the poison of realism and the filthy, shapeless and miserable writing that goes under the name of "dialect" and that is nothing but "patois".' Kitchener then outlined his dream:

> I should like more than anything for a responsible company to take hold of [*Meini Gwagedd*] and to marry it [either to the stage or to dramatic recitation]. It was a bit of a blasphemy, but consciously so on my part, to construct a drama containing elements of melodrama throughout, and one that was wholly static, depending entirely on the power of words and on the excitation of atmosphere that comes from within the writing, and not from external action, or from the usual stagey accidents. Things that have happened, and not things that are happening or to happen – it is of these that the drama speaks, and speak it does rather than living them in acts and deeds on stage – and that's the challenge that inheres in my bit of a tale, *as a drama*.[23]

For the Lampeter performance, the Cardiganshire drama and music committees combined to create an elite company capable of mounting a multi-media production. The wailing Hebrew music of Max Bruch, the back-cloth and stage scenery painted by the distinguished young artist John Elwyn (Davies), the lighting effects overseen by a professional from the New Theatre, Cardiff – all these were treated as integral to the complex attempt to realize the play's atmospheric meanings through stage performance, and the hand-picked cast was directed by Mary Lewis, a talented and highly experienced producer who was a friend of the author. Also integral to the production were the discussions of *Meini Gwagedd*'s meaning initiated and orchestrated by the producer and in which it was intended the audience should also participate at the conclusion of the performance, although this did not in fact happen.

Instead, the production was widely discussed in the press, and the reports offer fascinating snapshots of the occasion, ranging from the chattering of the audience that prevented the prologue music from creating the desired atmosphere, to hitches in what remained an amateur production, such as mistiming the lighting effects and the untimely appearance of ghostly shadows on the backcloth. In miniature, these are perfect examples of the dilemma facing Kitchener as a Welsh-language dramatist. He lacked the drama workshop or studio theatre that would probably have best served the most urgent and profound of his creative needs, theatres like the one Saunders Lewis was to establish for his private purposes at Garthewin, or like the Gate Theatre in London that had briefly (through Emlyn Williams) indicated a vague interest in staging an English version of *Cwm Glo* – a proposal that proved as sadly chimerical as that (mentioned by D. R. Davies in a letter to Kitchener) to turn the play into a Hollywood film.

Kitchener's letter to Mary Lewis after the production is masterly in every respect. Beginning by thanking her, with evident sincerity and humility, for staging *Meini Gwagedd* he then proceeded to a brilliant commentary on both the play and its performance in Lampeter. The question whether the work was poem or play no longer interested him, he confessed. What he was now confident of, was that it could provide a powerful theatrical experience, and it was in any case high time for a Welsh audience to have something difficult with which to wrestle:

> I hope that there was no-one in the theatre that oppressively hot Saturday who *understood* every aspect of the play, after a single hearing – or else its interest will quickly be exhausted. Truly great literary works break new ground every time they are produced, else why do people long used to masterpieces keep returning to them, time after time? It is not the function of theatre to provide exhaustively for the intelligence, as does a dictionary, but rather to

create a field of sensibility – to create an *emotional intelligence* that is more than the sum of the petty 'understandings' of the intellect.

He had, he confessed, come to a different understanding of his own play through being in the Lampeter audience. He had himself conceived of the father as

> a kind of *Fury* to whom there could be no reconciling, full of fire and passion, and with a reserve of feeling and of voice that gradually swelled to a storm of sounding language, a tempest of internal rending, of pride, of boastfulness, and of unyielding malicious resentment. So, likewise, it is with his daughters – they too squirming under the heavy weight of their father's anger, and yet at the same time exulting in their role as agents of fate.

Mary Lewis, however, had convincingly conceived of the three in terms of 'muted emotion', and of 'a constant, cold, melancholic, *beaten, fated*' kind of passion. He wished, though, that her production had been able to distinguish more clearly between the animated, earthy quality of the Four's bickerings (and here he commended her decision to allow them to move occasionally, as he had always assumed they would) and the fixed, wholly static quality of the Three, as if their mode of speaking suggested a 'Stylistic Statuary'. He had imagined them as 'an un-realistic Chorus, shrouded in fate like a fog – being beyond fussing with realistic details, being as eternal as mist on a mountain-top or hoar frost on the sunless side of the Rhondda valley . . . fixed silhouettes against a changeful sky'.

Kitchener concludes by explaining that the inescapable black oppressiveness of the play originated in his original vision of the dreadful and distressing economy of the bog, a fearsome instance of the decay of Welsh rural life. His comment is a reminder that intimately personal though the charge of psychic feeling surging through the text of *Meini Gwagedd* may be, the play is also tolling the knell of rural Wales and thereby elegizing the decline and fall of western civilization. Shortly before writing *Meini Gwagedd* Kitchener wrote a letter confessing that a book he had recently read had so alarmed him with its diagnosis of the West that it had left 'the most appalling Question Mark in [his] mind'. He was referring to *Adfeilion* (Ruins), a trenchant attempt by a young academic, Alwyn D. Rees, to find the appropriate intellectual and moral means of combating the pessimistic view of the West's terminal decline taken by essentially determinist writers such as Spengler, with whose diagnosis of the contemporary malaise Rees was nevertheless fundamentally in sympathy. The thinkers to whom Rees turns for remedy are Chesterton, Berdyaev, Barth, Maritain and Christopher Dawson, who believe that religion alone can restore a mad world to its senses; and Reinhold Niebuhr's views are eloquently cited in this connection: 'Without the ultrarational hopes and passions of religion, no society will have the courage to conquer despair and attempt the impossible . . . The truest visions of religion are illusions, which may be partly realised by being resolutely believed' (*Adfeilion*, Llyfrau'r Dryw, 1943, p. 39).

The whole of Kitchener's heroically active life was lived in the energetic belief that the things that must be changed could be changed, however absurdly impossible it might seem to pessimists and determinists – that the decline of the Welsh language and culture could be arrested and reversed; that industrial society could be dismantled; that social life would again be informed by spiritual values; in short that, to borrow the powerful image from *Buchedd Garmon*, the swine might yet be ejected from the vineyard. And, on one level, this is exactly what *Meini Gwagedd* is saying, as it implicitly condemns the characters for talking themselves everlastingly out of acting; for mouthing about fate whereas the responsibility really lies with them for their own moral and spiritual collapse. But there is also the dark undertow to the text as the rip currents of Kitchener's psyche draw him back, sucking him down into the depths of his fear of an unlocatable past's fateful pull. And his best work as a writer seems to be generated by the emotional dynamics of this intolerable dialectic between fate and free will. Kitchener did find a synthesis, however, for this thesis and antithesis, in his belief in a Calvinist God whose certain yet unknowable acts of predestination nevertheless set man free to act meaningfully as a moral agent. This God was the opposite of the evilly possessive father of *Meini Gwagedd* (a composite, perhaps, of his feelings towards both his parents), whose accursed spirit, like that of the bog, totally destroyed his descendants.

It is his religious faith that allows Kitchener to come to terms with the travails of his time of war in *Ing Cenhedloedd* (The Anguish of Nations), a three-part poem composed for the local eisteddfod at Treorci in 1945. It is formally laid out as a debate, the Thesis being the vulgar Darwinian argument that man is nothing but a creature of blind instinct, driven willy-nilly to acts of bloody destruction and self-destruction by the brutal laws of the evolutionary process. The Antithesis to this is the proposition that man is the puppet of pre-ordained Progress, and that his suffering is an inconsequential result of the remorseless advance of the juggernaut of history towards its sublime ends. The Synthesis is the assertion that in every believing Christian it is the soul, refashioned by grace in Christ's own image, that redeems the will, enabling it to knit the instincts together into an impregnable defence against evil. The Christian still suffers, of course, but that suffering is transfigured by the knowledge that God, in Christ, chose freely to shed the immunities of His divine nature in order to share fully the sufferings of human flesh, thereby delivering the believer from evil.

Kitchener uses three very different verse forms in order to lend appropriate character, and dramatic 'voice', to each of these arguments. The cynical nihilism of the Thesis is conveyed through the nervous energy of a helter-skelter verse with a glib pattern of rhyme; the callous blandness of the Antithesis is suggested by an expansive verse pattern and smugly confident rhythms; while the Synthesis is written in the form of a warmly intimate devotional hymn. Throughout, the poetry displays the extraordinary range and richness of Kitchener's lexicon, with much of the vocabulary, and many of the images, being drawn from his Tregaron experiences. Moreover, it is his early experience of losing a mother in childbirth that surely lies behind those passages in the Thesis where the sinister internal connection between life, suffering and death is blackly imaged in terms of birth throes, and where it is sardonically noted that 'across the doors of women's wombs is scrawled "Hic / iacet – here lies"'. There is a sense, therefore, in which Kitchener gives voice, in the Thesis to *Ing Cenhedloedd*, to the temptation to nihilism that his precocious experience of life's arbitrary cruelty had made a part of his very nature.

That said, *Ing Cenhedloedd* remains an unsatisfactory poem, repetitious, showy, verbose, even bombastic at times – weaknesses that are avoided in Kitchener's other long poem of the same period, *Yr Arloeswr* (The Pioneer), based on an experimental use of metres from the poetry of William Williams (Pantycelyn) and entered for competition in the Mountain Ash National Eisteddfod of 1946. In the first part, man, supposed master of the laws of progress, confidently sets about using his human reason to create a better world (imaged in terms of taming a wilderness into a family homestead). The humanist speaker consistently secularizes religious language to suggest the way the old superstitious belief in God, and in original sin, has been superceded by an enlightened scientific rationalism. But as the poem proceeds, so the humanist finds the wilderness over-running the clearing he has made, as his reason becomes entangled in rationalisation, and self-confidence obscures sight of the true self. Once the reason, that has renounced religious belief, begins to founder, Descartes's famous proposition, *Cogito, ergo sum*, is perverted into the bleak conclusion 'I know nothing, therefore I am not'. Nevertheless, still determinedly convinced that man is perfectible, ruthless humanism continues to torture and destroy human beings in the name of progress. Too late, the humanist learns that what he thought was the dawn of a new age is in fact the blood-red sunset of human judgement.

The second part opens with the penitent humanist dreaming of recovering his faith in the previously despised imagination, and of seeing the world as represented in fairy tales, legends and romances, where the sun arises triumphantly fresh every morning, the victor ludorum of the firmament. But the fairy tales also warn that the blessings of transfigured vision are to be secured, and kept, only on the strangest conditions; there can be no treasure that is not guarded by dragons. And that is the understanding to which the pioneer clings when he wakes from his dream and returns to the plot he had cultivated but that has now once again reverted to wilderness. Humbled, he vows to recognize that the beauty of life is inseparable from the inalienable mystery of its supra-human provenance; and further to accept that he can never, of his own free human will, eradicate the evil in himself. He realizes he can truly come into his own only *in extremis*, when he has given himself passionately, wholly and irrevocably to a power whose demands seem unreasonable and absurd to ordinary human understanding; and when he has vilified and renounced everything that is usually cherished as worthwhile.

Yr Arloeswr clearly prefigures *Sŵn y Gwynt sy'n Chwythu* in that it is a poem about the making of a saint – that is, in Calvinist terms, one who has been transformed by God's inexplicable grace and no longer lives by the light of ordinary human comprehension.[24] The poem also prefigures *Sŵn y Gwynt* by establishing an intimate, if indeterminate, connection between the spiritual crisis with which *Yr Arloeswr* is concerned and traumatic episodes in Kitchener's past. For example 'y llain', the Welsh word for a plot of land, connects the humanist's attempt in Part One to make a home for himself and his family out of the wilderness with Kitchener's resentment at his father's sale of the family smallholding, Y Llain, that had been lovingly fashioned out of bogland. Thus when, in Part Two, the humanist-turned-saint exchanges the 'llain' for the 'llan' (church), it is tempting to read this as related to a wish by Kitchener to transform (psychoanalysis might say 'sublimate') his long-repressed anger at the injustice of his father's action into an acceptance of God's unfathomable will. Similarly, mother images seem to carry a psychic charge as well as having spiritual meaning. God's act of grace in saving the sinner by violently separating him from the sinful world is likened to the way a baby is born by being violently separated from its mother. Here again there are implied connections with Kitchener's early experience, as it is insisted that every birth entails a rupture as intense as dying.

Yr Arloeswr is a powerful and unjustly neglected poem, a remarkable demonstration of Kitchener's uncanny affinity with the work of William Williams, Pantycelyn. And this is much more than merely a matter of imitating metre, rhyme-scheme and rhythm; it is a case of Kitchener's instinctively grasping the whole psycho-spiritual gestalt of Pantycelyn's great eighteenth-century epic of the soul, *Theomemphus*. But in the end, there is still just a hint of pastiche about *Yr Arloeswr*, and while the allegorical method Kitchener adopts from William Williams (and the Bible) does allow him to treat the experience as typical rather than personal, it also makes the narrative rather remote and dated. It would be another six years before Kitchener would again enter the vale of soul-making, in *Sŵn y Gwynt sy'n Chwythu*, and by then he had developed the means of translating Pantycelyn's psycho-spiritual poetry into his own distinctively modern and confessional terms.

Chapter IV

Such is the power of *Sŵn y Gwynt sy'n Chwythu*, and such a compaction is it of Kitchener's vital energies, that it is tempting to treat all that happened in the few years remaining to him after the war as a preparation for the writing of that one incomparable poem. And so, in one important sense, indeed it was. But it was also a time of accelerating activity, and achievement, in public life. His political convictions had continued to develop through the writing of *Meini Gwagedd* and *Ing Cenhedloedd*. Not only had he attacked the Darwinist ethos of raw capitalism, and the totalitarian regimes born of utopian fascist and communist ideology, he had also warned against the sinister anti-democratic creep of bureaucracy he had witnessed in Britain during the Depression of the thirties and feared it would proceed apace in a post-war welfare state. In such an engineered and centrally regulated society, Welsh-language culture would be treated as an inconvenient anomaly, a point Kitchener made in a wartime letter about the Ministry of Food's failure to produce Welsh-language ration coupons. A similarly dismissive attitude to Welsh by the National Union of Teachers, recommending the language should not be taught in Rhondda schools, also enraged him.

Kitchener's view of himself as the heir of the Welsh Radical tradition came to the fore in his 1945 General Election campaign as Plaid Cymru candidate in Rhondda East (Rhondda Fach), where he faced, in W. J. Mainwaring, a sitting MP of impeccable Labour credentials – Central Labour College educated, with a strong track record as a union official. 'Central Whitehall planning for Wales' would, Kitchener predicted, result from a Labour victory. Socialism in power would enhance the 'tendency to executive dictatorship'. When he tried his luck in Rhondda

West (Rhondda Fawr) in the 1950 and 1951 General Elections, his Labour opponent was the virulently anti-nationalist Iorwerth (Iorrie) Thomas, whose election leaflets characteristically warned that 'the policy of the Welsh Nationalist Party would lead to civil war, bloodshed and years of constant strife with our English-speaking friends across the border'. In reply, Kitchener argued that his was a nationalism based on Christian and democratic principles and infused with the spirit of true internationalism, which respected the right of all nations to self-government. The contempt in which Rhondda Labour held such a politically puny party became apparent at the end of the count, when Iorrie Thomas quietened his supporters' jeering chant 'Go home little man' by appealing for fair play for his plucky opponent: 'Let the little man speak.'

These were, then, years of indefatigable political campaigning, with Kitchener and his co-workers travelling the length (but not breadth) of the Rhondda, one hand on the wheel of an Austin Seven, the other holding a not infrequently defective microphone. Instinctively a man of the theatre, Kitchener relished the carnivalesque side of politics – the zany escapades, the odd encounters, the manic scheming. His high spirits and zest for eye-catching campaigns continued unabated into early middle age. He is reputed to have been one of the intrepid band at the Dolgellau National Eisteddfod (1949) that scaled the church tower to pull down the Union Jack and run up the Welsh Dragon. One of the wild Tregaron Georges to the last, it might seem, yet his was a respected moderating influence within the Plaid Cymru of that time, mediating between the conservative and radical wings of the party.

He also retained his ability to be both combative and disarming, and to make friends with the most unlikely companions, such as H. W. J. Edwards from Trealaw, the eccentric Welsh Conservative and Catholic who literally became a fellow-traveller of Kitchener's on his campaign trails. Edwards's memory of their first meeting is worth recording:

We first met outside a Welsh Nationalist committee room in Tonypandy when I was introduced to him by a Nationalist agent who assured Mr Davies that it was quite useless to ask a Tory like myself to vote for him or for any Nationalist.

At the word Tory, 'Kitch's' eyes lit up. He rolled the word round his mouth to bring out the full Cardigan 'r'. He beamed at me as if I were a long lost friend, though indeed Kitch's political activities might fairly be summed up in terms of the bitterest hostilities to the 'Tories'.

'There are Tories and Tories,' he commented.

I looked ready for more.

'There are Tories and there are Conservatives. Which are you?'

Now this distinction is known only to a silent few and I had to make some quick readjustments.

'Oh, I'm a Tory.'

'I suppose you're an admirer of the Stuarts?'

'Why, yes, I certainly am.'

'Hmmm. Did you ever hear of the Distributist League?'

'Yes, I did. I was a member.'

'The Distributist League converted me to Nationalism.'

'Did it? My Toryism converted me to Distributism.'

'In that event you will vote Nationalist.'

'Will I?'

We shook hands and that was that.[25]

Taking advantage of the clause in the 1944 Education Act that allowed County Councils to create Welsh-medium schools where there was demonstrable demand, Kitchener and others began a campaign to establish such a school in the Rhondda. After half a dozen years of knocking doors, fund-raising, public meetings and political agitation, success came in the form of a school for each of the two valleys, Ynys-wen (37 initial intake) in Rhondda Fawr, opening just three months ahead of Pontygwaith (13 initial intake) in Rhondda Fach. It was a development that would help reshape the Rhondda culturally and politically over the next half-century, and it resulted in Kitchener being honoured, after his death, as the leader of what had been little short of a revolutionary movement. For him, however, the revolution was far from over, as he argued passionately for the creation of a complete Welsh-medium education system, from primary schooling through secondary schools to a Welsh-medium university college. Welsh was not, he emphasized in a forthright *Herald of Wales* article (1951), a language of hearth and home and religious experience only; or a drawing-room accomplishment like piano-playing. Nor was it taught in schools simply as an ancient tongue with a 'lovely literature'. 'It is taught because it is adequate to the full life of those who use it.' No doubt remembering his own experience of raising three daughters in the Rhondda, he objected to those who exclaimed, 'Oh, isn't it lovely to hear them talk in Welsh'. The language was not cute or charming; 'The Welsh language, like every other, is because it is' (p. 1).

Kitchener's furious energy can at times seem almost frightening. A teacher by profession, he was also a lay-preacher, a teacher of evening classes, a frequent newspaper columnist, a lecturer at summer schools, almost a full-time politician, an insatiable reader, a broadcaster, and a man still obsessed by literature and drama – his Pandy Players acted *Meini Gwagedd* under his direction, and he continued to play a key role in the drama movement throughout Wales. And on top of all this was his quite unreasonable passion for gardening – so remarkable was it that it attracted admiring but somewhat baffled comment from all his friends, and found its way into *Sŵn y Gwynt sy'n Chwythu*. It was a signature act, and his garden a landscape sculpture. Not content with cultivating the moderately large plot adjoining Aeron, Kitchener spent all his 'spare' time turning the arid land that sloped down behind the house to the valley bottom into a veritable hanging garden of Babylon, crafted into terraces by a descending series of dry stone walls. What on earth did such a manifestly superfluous activity mean? *Sŵn y Gwynt* certainly confirms that Kitchener himself was well aware of its peculiar, personal, symbolic significance. But probably, like any work of art, it meant more than he could possibly tell by any other means. It was a creative act of defiance and a defiant act of

Mair and Kitchener, with, from the left, Megan, Manon and Mari, on holiday at Pantyfedwen, Borth, Ceredigion, 1951.

creativity – asserting the value of beauty in the very face of physical ugliness; reclaiming the Rhondda for nature; producing an unlikely rhyme between the rural landscape of Tregaron and the industrial landscape of Trealaw; saving a vineyard from the swine; keeping the creeping convolvulus of political disorder and psychological despair at bay; and deeper than all, perhaps, redeeming the anger that called for vengeance at the loss of his true inheritance, Y Llain, by harnessing it to produce his own incomparable triumph of a llain (plot). In the interviews his sister Tish gave shortly before her death, she repeatedly recalled that Y Llain had been turned, through their father's loving care, into an Edenic garden.

In the autumn of 1947, Kitchener became involved in the struggle to prevent the War Office from commandeering 27,000 acres of land, including 30 farms and the ruins of the great Cistercian Abbey at Strata Florida. And this near the town named after the gentle Caron, the shepherd who became a Celtic saint, and exactly a century after Henry Richard, MP for Tregaron, had been made secretary of the international Peace Society. Such a manoeuvre by the War Office, following the failure of a similar attempt in the Preseli, confirmed Kitchener in his view that a London government would always ruthlessly persist in implementing its centralist policies until it overpowered all Welsh opposition ('the King never dies'). In an impassioned essay, he wrote of how anger and hatred coursed through his blood and poisoned his brain when he saw this bayonet being thrust into the land of his heart and into the heartland of Welsh-language culture. The proposal was to turn the ancient sanctuary of Christian civilization into a military garrison, and in praying that this might not happen Kitchener used his essay to tell a rosary of personal and historical reminiscences.

Some four years later, with Trawsfynydd now the military target, Kitchener twice travelled the long road north in his little Austin Seven to link arms with the protesters who were among the first in Britain to adopt Gandhi's tactics of non-violent resistance. The second time, his wife tried to dissuade him from going, as he was clearly unwell; during the journey back, the stomach pains became so severe he had to stop the car and ask his passenger to drive home in his stead. Cancer of the colon was diagnosed, requiring treatment that involved long periods of hospitalization, and it was while he was in East Glamorgan Hospital, Church Village (near Pontypridd) that Kitchener composed *Sŵn y Gwynt sy'n Chwythu* in his head and dictated it section by section to his wife. It was broadcast in January, 1952, and again in August of that year, just a few days before Kitchener's death on 25 August.

Whether or not Kitchener actually realized he was dying when he was writing *Sŵn y Gwynt sy'n Chwythu*, it has all the hallmarks of the traditional deathbed poem. The speaker's situation is, as

Seamus Heaney observed of a poem by Yeats, 'that of somebody *in extremis*, somebody who wants to make his soul, to bring himself to wholeness, to bring his mind and being into congruence with the divine mind and being'.[26] From the beginning, an Eliotesque image suggests that, by dislocating the usual sense of life, the chill hospital becomes the disconcerting site of memory:

> Today,
> there came a breeze thin as the needle of a syringe,
> cold, like ether-meth on the skin,
> to whistle round the other side of the hedge.
> For a moment, I felt a numbness in my ego,
> like the numbness of frost on the fingers of a child
> climbing the stiles of Y Dildre and Y Derlwyn to school . . .
> But the hedge is thick-trunked, and high,
> and its shelter firm so that nothing comes through it,
> – nothing at all but the sound of the wind that is blowing.
>   (Translated by Joseph P. Clancy, p. 109)

That wind may be thought of as the reality principle, and throughout the poem Kitchener unflinchingly confronts what he regards as his lifelong failure to face up to reality. This is where the voices come in. He peoples his poem, so to speak, with the many accusatory voices of his conscience. But he also hears contrary voices, the tempting voices of internal reassurance; the voices that tell him to take no notice of conscience. So the poem unfolds like a modern version of an old morality play.

The first voice mocks him by recalling how, as a very little boy attending his mother's funeral, he had learned to act a part; how he had pretended to grieve in order to avoid really, feelingfully, registering the early deaths in his family and his neighbourhood. Then Kitchener's own voice re-enters the poem to recall, nostalgically, how safe he had felt as a child on the farm, protected from the wind's harm by the stout hedges planted by his father and forefathers. A temptingly reassuring voice is next heard persuading him that he was nevertheless not a coward; instead of cowering in this boyhood refuge he had courageously courted the wind by climbing the tall trees. Similarly later, so this voice continues, he braved the hostile fury of life in the Rhondda of the locust years. He helped in the soup kitchens, joined in the jazz carnivals and the games of football between striking miners and policemen. He had even displayed a kind of reckless courage in taking on all comers by preaching Welsh nationalism on street corners. Briefly persuaded by the truths spoken by this flattering voice, Kitchener himself at this point joins in the hymn of self-praise, only for another voice to erupt impatiently into the poem, accusing him of vanity and self-pity. This pitiless voice unmasks the secret satisfaction he had derived from acting the hero; and it rubs his nose in the evident uselessness of all the work he'd done in the Rhondda.

This is the turning point in the poem. His core of selfhood having been completely demolished, Kitchener is now able to turn to God in utter weakness, and in complete selflessness. This is, of course, a precondition of the visitation of grace. God reveals Himself at this critical juncture by bringing to Kitchener's mind the episode at the very end of the gospel according to John when Peter is minded to forget the crucified Christ and to return to his fishing. All night he and his friends trawled for fish, but caught nothing. But come the dawn, they spied a figure on the shore who advised them to cast their nets on the other side; whereupon they caught fish in abundance, and Peter recognized that he had been brought into redemptive, life-altering communion with the risen Christ.

For Kitchener, this story (which he, as a lay-preacher, had previously taken as the text of what became his favourite sermon) seems to be an allegory of his own life. He sees the whole of his past life, although ostensibly devoutly Christian, as a spiritual sham; an evasion of reality; a repeated denial of Christ. But he remains terrified of being possessed by the only true reality – the reality of God's grace that, like the wind, 'bloweth where it listeth'. It alone can bring Christian salvation, but it does so only by crucifying, through its divine, non-human 'otherness', all that man humanly cherishes, all that man naturally lives by, as Saunders Lewis had devastatingly demonstrated in *Amlyn ac Amig*, the chilling play on which Kitchener partly modelled his own self-understanding. Hence his great, despairing cry to God, at the conclusion of the poem, to pity him, to spare him, to refrain from making him a saint, in the Calvinistic sense (as used in *Yr Arloeswr*) of an elect soul violently seized and saved by grace:

> 'Quo vadis, quo vadis,' where are you going?
> Stop pursuing me to Rome, to a cross, my head towards the
> >> ground.
>   O Saviour of the lost,
> save me, save me, save me,
> from Your baptism that washes the Old Man so clean;
> keep me, keep me, keep me,
> from the inevitable martyrdom of Your elect.
> Save me and keep me
> from the wind that is blowing where it will.
> So be it, Amen
>   and Amen. (Translated by Joseph P. Clancy, p. 119)

The greatness of these lines lies in their doubleness of meaning – the way they simultaneously cry out for salvation and decry it. They perfectly capture a soul perhaps suspended permanently in spiritual limbo, but also perhaps glimpsed in transit between what St Paul would call the Old Man and the New Man.

As a poem concerned with 'the problem of making a saint', *Sŵn y Gwynt* was, for Kitchener, a development from *Yr Arloeswr* and the third part of *Ing Cenhedloedd*, as he explained in a letter to his friend Aneirin Talfan Davies, who had commissioned the poem for broadcast in a series of Welsh-language poems by younger poets. And the poem is very consciously constructed with the radio in mind, as Kitchener, who had had considerable experience of broadcasting by 1952, followed Saunders Lewis in believing that the new medium offered Welsh poetry significant new opportunities for development. It encouraged the writing of a new 'cerdd dafod', an oral poetry in the old Welsh tradition, and it thus encouraged the use of a natural, colloquial Welsh, instead of debased dialect – a development that would benefit both poet and dramatist. 'The modern poet', he wrote in 'Poet's View' (*The Herald of Wales*), 'must master the machines of the twentieth century. He must subdue the mike. As the sixteenth century stage evolved its giant Shakespeare, so radio today must produce microphone poets of stature' (p. 7). There was also a different issue of language. Radio had so far been dominated by the language of 'the politician, the preacher, the propagandist; it would be good to hear the poet discussing the modern world, and good to give heed to his prophetic words' (p. 7). And Kitchener agreed with his friend Aneirin Talfan Davies (who, almost ten years earlier, had encouraged Dylan Thomas to write *Quite Early One Morning* for Welsh radio, the precursor of *Under Milk Wood*) that radio could be used to sustain and extend the existing popular audience for poetry: 'As the Eisteddfod is still the national holiday of our common folk, so radio poetry is their evening's entertainment' (p. 7).

Kitchener believed that, by making poems available and accessible to 'ordinary minds', radio could overcome popular prejudice against modernist poetry. He also hoped that in an age when publishers were interested only in short lyrics, Aneirin Talfan Davies's experiment could help re-establish 'the long poem which turns the poet's mind from his introverted self to an objective description and analysis of contemporary tendencies' (p. 7). What worried him, however, about the poems that preceded his own in the series was that they were so melancholic: 'the poets view the world through a death's head's empty socket' (p. 7). And this was because they mourned the triumph of the modern age and elegized the passing of a rural community. Much though he admired J. M. Edwards's broadcast poem, he felt uneasy that 'each line in [his] description of his native Cardiganshire village is replete with "hiraeth"; a longing for the life that used to be . . . It is a village that has died, for the treachery of the wind blows like a sly breeze across the frontier, and the loveliness that was is withered' (p. 7).

The sound of that wind is to be heard in *Sŵn y Gwynt sy'n Chwythu*, but so is the sound of Shelley's turbulently revivifying west wind (the poem was one Cassie Davies particularly remembered from her days at Tregaron County School) and of R. Williams Parry's 'Cymru 1937', which famously concludes by petitioning the fierce wind to drive an apathetic people to a moment of real existential choice: 'blow [them] to the synagogue or blow [them] to the pub.' Then there are also echoes of Eliot's poetry ('What is the wind doing . . .?') and perhaps of T. H. Parry Williams's east wind, the 'lost breath' that 'floors mortals in its course / To show man what wind is'. That Kitchener's image is a composite of all these and more is not surprising, as *Sŵn y Gwynt* is an extraordinary compound of so much that Kitchener had read, as well as a forum for several different states of mind.

Indeed, the idea and structure of such a forum may well itself have come, at least in part, from Kitchener's reading. By the late forties, he had come to regard Saunders Lewis's newspaper reviews of the Welsh plays produced at the 1919 Swansea Drama Festival as having a canonical status, and one of the comments made by Lewis had been that 'the theatre might well return to the elementary pageant of the medieval mystery and miracle plays . . . there is in these an austerity, a reticent economy of emotion which are the qualities that we so grievously lack' (quoted in script of *Y Ddrama Gymraeg*). This tied in with Kitchener's developing interest in the way drama in Wales had begun in the churches, from which the morality play had emerged and survived, in popular secular form, down to the eighteenth-century Interludes of Twm o'r Nant. At that point it had actually resumed its original religious character in William Williams's *Theomemphus* and had thereafter both influenced nineteenth-century pulpit rhetoric and assumed yet another shape in the little moralistic dialogues performed in Nonconformist chapels and printed in religious periodicals. In adopting a morality play structure in *Sŵn y Gwynt sy'n Chwythu*, Kitchener was therefore doing several things; consciously working in what he believed to be an authentically Welsh dramatic tradition;

deliberately creating a modern Welsh religious drama in a form deriving from the Middle Ages (an achievement for which, he had suggested in a radio discussion [*Y Ddrama Gymraeg*], W. J. Gruffydd was uniquely well equipped); and even half-consciously complying with his friend Aneirin Talfan Davies's stated wish for a radio drama that would rival the great Welsh preachers' theatrical ability to enact the eternal struggle between evil and good for possession of the human soul. (It may be no accident that Kitchener actually includes a portion of one of his own sermons in the body of his poem.)[27]

In his effort to write the history of his own inner life in the form of a morality play, Kitchener may have been assisted by John Ellis Williams's recent innovative production of Tegla Davies's Welsh adaptation of Bunyan's *Pilgrim's Progress*. Such a creative convergence of Welsh-language and English-language materials was certainly consonant with Kitchener's own practice, as his deep interest in T. S. Eliot's religious drama blended with his passion for the plays of Saunders Lewis. He had clearly taken the advice Lewis had proffered young Welsh poets at Llandybïe, to read the Eliot of 'Little Gidding' (later to form part of *Four Quartets*), with his melancholy contempt for modern man's attempt to find refuge from spiritual realities in the nullity of frenzied activity. As for *The Family Reunion* (1939), it sees conscience as 'the cancer / that eats away the self'; and it brings the soul to 'the stone passages / Of an immense and empty hospital / Pervaded by a smell of disinfectant'. *The Cocktail Party* (1949), actually mentioned in *Sŵn y Gwynt*, deals with a situation where the self has become 'a set of obsolete responses'; it specifically uses the experience of hospitalization as metaphor, since 'stretched on the table, / You are a piece of furniture in a repair shop / For those who surround you, the masked actors; / All there is of you is your body / And the "you" is withdrawn'; and it balks at trying to understand the process of 'transhumanisation', the suffering on the way of illumination.

There is also *Murder in the Cathedral* (1935), an earlier play but an active influence on Welsh writers in the early fifties, following a translation by Thomas Parry that Kitchener reviewed in 1950, and a broadcast produced by Aneirin Talfan Davies. The morality play format, the anguished prayers, all are important aspects of a religious drama in which a chorus of 'common people' speak of themselves as ones 'Who fear the blessing of God, the loneliness of the night of God, the surrender required, the deprivation inflicted; / Who find the injustice of men less than the justice of God' and are therefore content to go on living, 'Living and partly living'. In Kitchener's masterly essay (1948) on Saunders Lewis's work there are a couple of brilliant pages comparing Lewis with Eliot, where it is suggested that Lewis's calm certainty of faith knows nothing of the 'terror at the broken souls of a shattered world' that is felt by an Eliot whose tempters in *Murder in the Cathedral* are powerfully real and whose agony of mind is inscribed in the nervous parallelisms of a verse that is always doubling back on itself.

That is a powerful characterization of Kitchener's own rhythm of writing in *Sŵn y Gwynt sy'n Chwythu*. But equally relevant to the poem are those pages in the essay on Saunders Lewis where he discusses *Amlyn ac Amig* (1940), the play whose action he prays, at the height of his poem's spiritual crisis, he may be spared from having to live out in his own life. That is because in *Amlyn ac Amig* the latter returns, a stranger and a leper, to the house of his friend, Amlyn, one Christmas Eve, to remind him of the holy vow they had once made as young knights never to deny each other anything. And now Amig has returned, at the Archangel Raphael's express command, to require Amlyn to kill his two young children so that he, Amig, might be washed clean of his leprosy in their blood. In an agony of soul, Amlyn agrees, but the 'divine comedy' ends with God miraculously sparing the children and returning them, on Christmas morning, to their grieving father. Clearly the play is meant to instance the utter 'otherness' of an Almighty who declared 'I AM THAT I AM'; beyond all good or evil; 'you cannot speak of God by speaking of man in a loud voice' insisted the neo-Conservative theologian, Karl Barth, whose work appealed to some Welsh ministers after the war. However, the deliberately cruel twist given to the parent-child relationship in *Amlyn ac Amig* must have had a disturbing resonance for Kitchener Davies.

What he notes in his essay, though, is that the play closely resembles one section of *Bywyd a Marwolaeth Theomemphus* (1764), William Williams Pantycelyn's astonishing 6,000-line epic of the psycho-spiritual struggle for salvation. Abasis, an ordinary man, had experienced religious conversion in his youth, but had then settled down to a happy, comfortable family life. Beloved by all, he had a good name, yet Pantycelyn wrote of him 'a man's name became his, he lost the name of saint'. Warned by Abasis's example, Theomemphus (the Christian hero) accepts that he has to undergo the purgatory of putting by Philomela, his wife, and of submitting entirely to the agonizingly absolute demands of God's grace.

Kitchener's almost obsessive interest in *Theomemphus* owed a lot to Saunders Lewis's remarkable *Williams Pantycelyn* (1927), the first instance in Welsh of a psychoanalytic reading of personality. So revolutionary was it that Lewis had to create Welsh terms for psychoanalysis, repression and sublimation; and the book was written just when Freud was being widely read for the first time in English intellectual circles, as the phenomenon of shell-shock persuaded the previously sceptical of the relevance of Freud's theories of the unconscious as the cellar of repressed passions and violently disturbing memories. However, Saunders Lewis had read not Freud but Professor Robert H. Thouless's *An Introduction to the Psychology of Religion*, a most unFreudian attempt to reconcile religion and psychoanalysis. And both *Williams Pantycelyn* and *Sŵn y Gwynt sy'n Chwythu* may be read as attempts to accomplish a similar synthesis.

Indeed, the phenomenon of (re)conversion in middle age, such as that of Theomemphus and Kitchener Davies, was of particular interest to Thouless, who interpreted the conversion experience as the disintegration and reintegration of the conscious self, the result of the eruption into consciousness of psychic elements previously tensely repressed and relegated to the unconscious.

Accordingly, Saunders Lewis sees Williams Pantycelyn as being a great poet of religious experience precisely because he was a pioneer poet of the stresses and strains of the individual psyche. He argues that, for Pantycelyn (as, perhaps, for Kitchener), poetry was actually a unique means of exploring the depths of the psyche and that such an exploration was imperative, because God was to be genuinely encountered only at the end of this inner journey. *Theomemphus* was thus written in the language, and to the unpredictable dictation, of the unconscious. And if poetry was for Pantycelyn, as Lewis saw it, a therapeutic practice that could promote spiritual health, then so was the Methodist *seiat* (by which Kitchener had been so transfixed at Llwynpiod). Lewis specifically terms the *seiat* 'the clinic of the soul', and compares the work done there to that done by psychotherapists. In both cases, passions that, if permanently repressed, would damage the psyche, are brought to conscious expression and may then be integrated into the conscious self, which is thereby both radically altered and strengthened. A Christian, says Lewis, would call this a spiritual transformation; whereas a modern 'scientific' psychoanalyst would describe it as the formation of a mature, self-disciplined personality.

Sŵn y Gwynt sy'n Chwythu, a product of Kitchener's lifelong fascination with the *seiat* at Llwynpiod, may usefully be regarded as 'the clinic of the soul'. In his autobiographical essay for radio, 'Adfyw' (1950), he had movingly admitted to having psychic wounds that needed healing, each of which was in some ways an aspect of the other:

> So high did land prices climb in that auction following the [First World] War that my father, poor man, accepted his fate and, instead of buying a farm, sold Y Llain and broke up the home. (Only three hurts, which I'll simply mention, have I experienced – the loss of my mother when I was six, the sale of Y Llain when I was eighteen, and minutely witnessing, when I was 27, the malicious cancer, like a convolvulus, choking the life out of the aunt who had raised me.)

By thus relegating the crucial passage to a parenthesis, he seems to be seeking to minimize its painful significance – one could not wish for a more striking textual instancing of the mechanism of repression.[28] The primal wound was obviously the loss of his mother when he was six, but although it was thus mentioned (parenthetically) in 'Adfyw', nowhere, before *Sŵn y Gwynt sy'n Chwythu*, had he allowed himself to feel the pain:

> Remember coming back in Tre-wern's trap
> from mother's funeral? You got to sit in the front seat
>   with Ifan
> and everyone felt sorry for you – a hero, so little, so
>   noble,
> Not everyone gets a chance to lose his mother at six,
>   and learn to act so early.
>   (Translation by Joseph P. Clancy, p. 110)

It is a heartrending passage because, after more than forty years, Kitchener can still approach that moment of loss only obliquely, through the protective device of savagely sarcastic self-accusation. But at least the subject is broached, and as the poem proceeds, it remorselessly, if implicitly, explores the consequences for the rest of his life of that initial and initiating moment of suppression of agony, of repression of feeling. To that moment, Kitchener attributes his subsequent compulsive passion for acting, both on the stage and in 'real life'. And as *Sŵn y Gwynt* proceeds, so this sense of having lived only a life of masquerade grows, until it devours every detail of Kitchener's existence – including, most piteously and terrifyingly, even his home life with his wife and his three lovely little daughters.

What it means for a small child to be separated from its mother first became apparent to psychoanalysts who studied wartime evacuees – and of course Kitchener was doubly an 'evacuee', in that the loss of his mother was followed by expulsion to distant foreign Banbury. They discovered that separation meant 'far more than than the actual experience of sadness', it could in fact 'amount to an emotional blackout'.[29] That expressive phrase encapsulates the way in which children who are prevented (like Kitchener) from mourning the loss of their mother, may spontaneously create a psychic defence against their unacknowledged pain by developing a 'false' personality insulated from their very deepest feelings. Such a defence may 'successfully' last a lifetime, but it leads to the person feeling inauthentic, a sham, a charlatan, an actor, an impostor – those very feelings to which Kitchener gives powerful voice in *Sŵn y Gwynt sy'n Chwythu* until, at the very end, his 'conversion' experience results in a breakdown of the constructed self; an event that is at once an agonizing crucifixion experience and an experience of liberation and salvation. Reliving his life, he realizes that the anger that had energized all his political work may not have been political anger only, but also a displaced expression of the anger that was at the heart of the grieving he had never allowed himself to experience for his mother. And his lifelong impulse to challenge, to defy, to shock – this was only a compulsively repeated substitution for that original, primal challenge he had failed to face, and was still terrified of facing; the inner challenge of facing up to the violent pain and anger at the loss of his mother.

And also at the other two losses of his life, the loss of Bodo, and the loss of his loved-and-hated father, whose death in 1945, more or less coinciding with the threat to Tregaron, may unconsciously have triggered Kitchener's psychic self-exploration. In fact, Bodo Mari's death is woven into the fabric of *Sŵn y Gwynt* through the recurrent image of the convolvulus, which links the slow strangling of her life by cancer (and what must this have meant to Kitchener as he struggled with his own cancer at Church Village?) to Kitchener's epic exploits as a gardener and to his heroic attempts to clear the Rhondda of its 'weeds'. As Susan Sontag has shown, in her discussion of the 'mythologizing' of disease, cancer had taken over from TB as an important metaphor by the fifties, and 'the passion that people [wrongly] think will give them cancer if they don't discharge it is rage'.[30]

Of the father who had effectively deprived him of his longed-for inheritance, Kitchener seems to speak only fondly in *Sŵn y*

Gwynt, remembering that glorious summer of 1911 when he had so proudly helped the skilled miner-carpenter to craft the hedge that would protect Y Llain from every wind. But, of course, it would be his father who would smash that very hedge. And how Y Llain became for Kitchener, the growing boy, a substitute for the mother he had lost is movingly suggested by the images in terms of which he remembers the place. Brother, sister, and Kitchener himself are all fondly recalled as huddled there safely, 'like the babes in the story hidden with leaves by birds', as the wild winds, 'like legions of spirits', were deflected safely up and over the cottage's tiles by the sheltering hedges. Even in winter, Kitchener would daringly climb the tall, naked trees, and perch high 'like raven on bough / your knees and arms riding the wood / and your eyes tight shut on the astonishing surge / like a babe rocked to sleep in its crib by the rocking'.

The sharp nub of Kitchener's memory of his father appears, however, not in *Sŵn y Gwynt sy'n Chwythu* but in 'Adfyw', where he recalls how, being so clumsily unskilled at his father's work, he cut himself with the miner's axe and a scar formed that still left its mark. What an image – deflecting his future anger at his father back towards himself; turning his father's future wounding of him into self-wounding; yet also making of it all a mark of initiation into manhood and a ritual act of wounding into song, since is he not implicitly admitting (like Glyn in 'Y Llysfam') that the loss of Y Llain, his expulsion from Eden, was the making of him as a poet-dramatist? No wonder he wrote a remarkable essay on scars in 1936: 'it is living sap that turns yesterday's wound into the scar of today . . . [and] today's scar lasts through tomorrow, the day after, and thereafter, and does not ever end.' The distorting echo of Paul's great letter to the Corinthians about love makes this passage a particularly suggestive one in Kitchener's case.

'A curse comes to being / As a child is formed. / In both, the incredible / Becomes the actual / Without our intention' (p. 108). Agatha's words in *The Family Reunion* apply, in different yet related ways, both to *Meini Gwagedd* (a play in which the

Eumenides are ominously omnipresent) and to *Sŵn y Gwynt*. As does her hope that 'The knot shall be unknotted / And the crooked made straight' (p. 108). In both works, too, we find 'A misery long forgotten, and a new torture, / The shadow of something behind our meagre childhood, / Some origin of wretchedness' (p. 102). But it is in *Sŵn y Gwynt sy'n Chwythu* only that Kitchener comes to the understanding reached by Harry in *The Family Reunion*:

> All this year,
> This last year, I have been in flight
> But always in ignorance of invisible pursuers.
> Now I know that all my life has been a flight
> And phantoms fed upon me while I fled. Now I know
> That the last apparent refuge, the safe shelter,
> That is where one meets them. That is the way of spectres.
> (p. 110)

Chapter V

> A fiery soul which, working out its way,
> Fretted the pigmy body to decay.

THE GREAT LINES FROM DRYDEN'S 'ABSALOM AND ACHITOPHEL' could provide one epitaph for Kitchener Davies, although they are not those his closest friends and acquaintances would probably have chosen. Instead, the reaction of many of them to his death was to turn him into a saint of a kind very different from the one Kitchener himself had in mind, and of which he would certainly not have approved. A hint of his probable reaction may be detected in his forthright comment on the way his friend, Rhydwen Williams, read the prayer with which *Sŵn y Gwynt sy'n Chwythu* ends. When Rhydwen visited the hospital the day after the first, January, broadcast, he was taken to task by Kitchener for reading the passage in so rhetorically sentimental a manner. Tears and self-pity were not allowed, said Kitchener; the clash of unyielding emotions in the lines was to be 'like steel on stone'. Kitchener – for whom *Sŵn y Gwynt* was, after all, an attempt to scour the soul clean of narcissism – regarded the approach of death in a similarly steely spirit, angered because there was still so much for him to do.

That remarkable prayer at the conclusion of *Sŵn y Gwynt sy'n Chwythu* naturally moved listeners enormously. Yet Saunders Lewis was resolutely unmoved by it when the poem shortly appeared in printed form, thanks to the initiative of Kitchener's friends, Gwenallt Jones and Aneirin Talfan Davies (who also arranged, in 1954, the broadcast of an English-language translation of the poem by Wil Ifan). Indeed, Lewis thought both the final sections of the poem inferior to the rest, objecting to the 'muddled theology' of the passage about Peter and to the derivative style of the climactic prayer. For him, the strength of the poem lay in the autobiographical aspects of the poem, regarded as an *apologia pro vita sua*. And he praised the juxtaposition of the strikingly different sections on Tregaron and the Rhondda, concluding with the suggestion that *Sŵn y Gwynt* was the poetic equivalent of the sobering paintings of the Rhondda then on display in a Cardiff art gallery. What is therefore interesting about Saunders Lewis's criticism is that it disregards the strictly religious part of the poem ('the problem of the making of a saint') and privileges instead the psycho-social aspects of *Sŵn y Gwynt*, the nightmare of that expulsion from Y Llain and the move to the Rhondda.

Kitchener Davies died in 1952, aged fifty. In 1953 Dylan Thomas died, aged 39. A year later, the controversial young minister and iconoclastic Welsh-language writer, Pennar Davies, dared to compare the two in *Dock Leaves*. Dylan Thomas was, he suggested,

> a gifted entertainer, a phenomenon in the history of twentieth-century publicity, and an interesting minor poet . . . if a literary critic is certain that Dylan Thomas is a far less important poet than the recently deceased Kitchener Davies, then it is his duty to say so, even if it might conceivably mean losing a few American tourists. (p. 36)

As Pennar Davies recognized, a cult was forming around Dylan Thomas; but what he did not recognize was that there was also a cult forming around Kitchener Davies. The two cults were, of course, very different, but there was a similarity, too, in that the image of the two poets fostered by their respective cults threatened to distort, or even to obscure, important aspects of the works they actually produced.

The myth at the centre of the cult of Kitchener Davies became all the more potent as it was fashioned in part by some of the most powerful Welsh-language writers of the post-war period – understandably so, since they had been his close friends and fellow-activists as well as fervent admirers of his talent. And to

*With Gwenallt (David James Jones) at the Plaid
Cymru Summer School, Dyffryn Ardudwy, 1949.*

speak of 'myth' is not to imply that their iconic portrait of 'Kitch' was a lie or a fantasy, but simply to suggest that the image they made out of their own intimate, and true, knowledge of the man was a partial one. Moreover, it was first selectively formed and then vigorously used and developed in order to serve a political agenda – a political agenda, incidentally, with which 'Kitch' himself would have been in complete sympathy.

Key poems in this myth-making process were those by Rhydwen Williams and Gwenallt. Rhydwen's 'Kitch' is a hymn, which, taking its cue from a tribute by Kate Roberts, treats Kitchener as a Christ-like, sacrificial redeemer figure driven by an excess of love for his Wales – 'And what if excess of love / Bewildered them till they died?', Yeats had written in 'Easter

1916' of the Irish freedom fighters. Gwenallt's 'Cwm Rhondda' is an elaborated version of the same vision, except that it weaves together phrases from *Sŵn y Gwynt sy'n Chwythu* to create an altogether more pugnacious rhetoric, depicting Kitchener as a peace-loving fighter against the massed forces that threatened his language and culture. And since Gwenallt's poem was written in the aftermath of Plaid Cymru's unexpected and stirring successes in the valleys, it is able to credit Kitchener with having set a revolution in motion. This is a theme also followed by Rhydwen Williams in his crown-winning sequence *Ffynhonnau* (1964), which celebrates the restoration to health in post-industrial Rhondda not only of the long-diseased natural landscape but also of the long-ailing Welsh language, thanks primarily to the Welsh-medium schools that Kitchener had fought to establish in the post-war years. And in 1989 one of those schools, Rhydfelen, staged its notable musical, *Kitch*, as a tribute to perhaps the greatest of those who had in effect been its founders.

Whilst it is understandable, and admirable, that these tributes should have been paid – their very number being testimony to Kitchener's remarkable impact – there is a danger that in the process sight may have been lost of the poignant complexity of his case and of his work. But there is one poem that intuitively homes in, like a heat-seeking missile, on Kitchener's inner world. In *Llwch*, a crown-winning poem (1986), the author, T. James Jones, spends a weekend snowbound in a hotel with his partner, Kitchener Davies's daughter, Manon Rhys. As time becomes eerily suspended, so intimate memories quietly gather like a snow drift (*lluwch*), or like the slow silent accumulation of ashes on ashes and dust on dust (*llwch*). And Manon Rhys's memories are of her father – how he died when she was so little; how he was buried in Llethr Ddu, the cemetery directly opposite Aeron, where the bereaved family continued to live; how one winter's night she'd dreamt he was still out there, and how she'd yearned to see him come home to the fire. And as Manon Rhys and T. James Jones seek the solace of pleasure in each other so, *Llwch* suggests in its conclusion, to love is to pay living tribute to the dead: 'Two pilgrims / buying a second / of loving familiarity / for fear . . . '

Nearly forty years after Kitchener's mortal remains were buried in Llethr Ddu, all his papers were reduced to ashes in the terrible conflagration on 11 April, 1990 that took the life of his widow, Mair, who had been such a devoted custodian of his memory and of his writings. It is all too cruelly literal an illustration of the truth of Theodore Zeldin's famous comment: 'History is a sieve that picks up only a small proportion of the debris of the past. What it salvages is, above all, books and manuscripts . . . What is honoured as literature is a "fragment of fragments".'

After the fire, charred scraps of manuscripts littered the hedgerows, awaiting any wind that blew and mocking any attempt to decipher the life they had once recorded. The occasional scrap did survive in legible form, a brand plucked from the burning, and in one such, black-edged by flame like a mourning card, D. J. Williams warns the friend whom he punningly addresses as 'Annwyl Geginydd' ('Dear Kitchen-er') that he can succeed in his applications for a teaching post in Cardiganshire only if he is willing to stoop to lobbying local councillors. It is unexpected evidence that in July 1935 (the date of the letter) he was seriously considering a return to his home county (perhaps because of his developing friendship with Mair Rees?). Who knows, therefore, what other scraps of information the fire consumed that may have significantly altered our picture of Kitchener Davies?

In his reminiscent essay, 'Adfyw' (1950), Kitchener used the fact that it would be broadcast simultaneously in Tregaron and in the Rhondda to help him hold the two different worlds of his existence in a single act of contemplation, as he was again to do two years later in another work written for radio, *Sŵn y Gwynt sy'n Chwythu*. For him, then, radio may indeed have been a medium for mediation. 'Today you are listening', he says to his Rhondda friends, 'Labour boys and redder boys, chapel boys

*James Kitchener Davies. This photograph was used on
Plaid Cymru leaflets during the 1950 and 1951 General Elections
in the Rhondda West constituency.*

and club boys', and he makes the occasion an opportunity to thank them all for what they have given him, a newcomer still: 'I am a stranger here; yonder is my native country.' And his love for that country swells to a diapason of praise to its memory:

Carving swamp alder into wooden spoons in front of the fire, plaiting switches into baskets in the barn, breathing the richness of the bullocks' manure as I clean out the calves' shed; being allowed to take Flower, the old one-eyed mare, and the cart to the main road for the first time, selling Seren and her calf, and walking the poor little thing two miles on her way, raising a pet pig from Spring to Christmas till he was tamer than a dog – then having to see, and hear, him being slaughtered for the house; catching a hare in a trap by the nails on its long hind legs and its cry filling the air – those are the things I remember when I remember. Those are the things and the people that shaped me, for better or for worse. (BBC text, 1950)

And then, returning to the same theme at the conclusion of the printed version of 'Adfyw' in *Poetry Wales*, he paints his birthplace in even richer tones of light and dark, this time touching even on the churchyard where his mother is buried:

From Llwynpiod to Llwynpia, from Rhydypandy to Tonypandy, thither ran my road. I can journey back along it any time I care – like looking back at the most glorious view in Wales, from the top of the Black Mountain down towards Llangadog, over the quilt of green leafy land – back to the Parish of Llanbadarn Odwyn where the chapel of Llwynpiod usurps the dignity of its church, except for the evening of Harvest Festival and the days of interment in consecrated earth.

Yes indeed, the spell of the coal pits was early determined to draw me to them; they claimed me; but the revenge of the country was like fate, and although I shall never again live naturally there, save as a visitor, it is still careful to govern me, to exile me, to place on me the mark of Cain in Cwm Rhondda. The roof of Y Llain has fallen; there are barren cattle on its hearths and its parlour is a dung heap – but it is Y Llain and its people and its things that insist on living, as revenants, in me tonight. (pp. 23–4)

In the Welsh, the fact that 'Llain' is a feminine noun means that it is the feminine spirit, so to speak, that dominates that final sentence of recollection.

To read the carefully altered epigraph from the Book of Job (Chapter 29) on Kitchener's simple tombstone in Llethr Ddu with 'Adfyw' in mind, is surely to appreciate its hauntingly enigmatic plainness:

> Fy ngwreiddyn oedd yn agored i'r dyfroedd, a'r gwlith a arhosodd yn fy mrig. (Job 29:19)
> (My root was spread out by the waters, and the dew still lies upon my branches.)

Notes

1. Seamus Heaney, 'Mossbawn', *Preoccupations* (London: Faber, 1995), p. 19.
2. Emrys Jones, 'Tregaron: the Sociology of a Market Town in Central Cardiganshire', in Elwyn Davies and Alwyn D. Rees (eds.), *Welsh Rural Communities* (Cardiff: University of Wales Press, 1960), p. 96.
3. R. J. Barker, *Christ in the Valley of Unemployment* (London: Hodder and Stoughton, 1936), p. 11.
4. *Christ in the Valley of Unemployment*, p. 37.
5. Gwyn Thomas, quoted in John Ormond, *Laughter Before Nightfall* (performance script, unpublished).
6. Saunders Lewis, 'My Country the Worst Hell in Europe Today', *The Welsh Nationalist* I: 5 (15 May 1932), 1.
7. George M. Ll. Davies, 'Ynysoedd Gobaith yng Nghymru', *Yr Efrydydd* VII, 9 (Mehefin, 1931), 240–6.
8. Quoted in Ceri W. Lewis, 'Hynt y Gymraeg yng Nghwm Rhondda', in Hywel Teifi Edwards (ed.), *Cwm Rhondda* (Llandysul: Gomer, 1995), pp. 72–125.
9. For a survey of the reactions to the staging of *Cwm Glo*, including most of the reactions quoted above, see 'Nid bachan budr yw Dai', in Hywel Teifi Edwards, *Arwr Glew Erwau'r Glo* (Llandysul: Gomer, 1994), pp. 143–212, and Manon Rhys, 'Atgyfodi *Cwm Glo*, Kitchener Davies', in Hywel Teifi Edwards (ed.), *Cwm Rhondda*, pp. 276–300.
10. Press quotation, April 1935, NLW, D. R. Davies Collection, Box 1. See also the programmes he chaired on *Y Ddrama Gymraeg* (NLW, BBC Scripts, Box 97).
11. Report of Kitchener's address at South Wales Social Service event, *Y Cymro* (11 Gorffennaf 1936); cf. 'Will 1936 Produce the Great Welsh Playwright?', *News Chronicle* (3 January 1936).
12. ' An analysis of present day Welsh literary effort', p. 31 and p. 32.
13. A collection of materials relating to the pageant movement can be found in NLW, D. R. Davies Collection, Box 2.
14. Translated by the author from *Buchedd Garmon*, in Ioan M. Williams (ed.), *Dramâu Saunders Lewis*, cyfrol I (Caerdydd: Gwasg Prifysgol Cymru, 1996), p. 139.

[15] Arnold P. Hinchcliffe, *Modern Verse Drama* (London: Methuen, 1977), p. 33.
[16] Quoted by newspaper announcing Kitch's forthcoming radio talk on Thursday evening, 18 April 1935 (NLW, D. R. Davies Collection, Box 1).
[17] Rhydwen Williams, 'James Kitchener Davies', *Poetry Wales* (Winter 1982), 61.
[18] Rhydwen Williams, 'Y Gŵr Bendigaid' (NLW, Rhydwen Williams Collection, 56).
[19] Quoted in Hywel Teifi Edwards (ed.), *Cwm Aman* (Llandysul: Gomer, 1996), p. 273.
[20] 'The Great Hunger', Patrick Kavanagh, *Collected Poems* (London: Martin Brian and O'Keeffe, 1972), pp. 3 and 55.
[21] Edward Thomas, 'Old Man', in *Collected Poems* (London: Faber, 1965 edition), pp. 104–5.
[22] W. B. Yeats, in a letter to Lady Gregory, quoted in Hinchcliffe, *Modern Verse Drama*, p. 19.
[23] Letter printed in the column by Euroswydd, *Y Faner* (13 Medi 1944). See NLW, D. R. Davies Collection, Box 1.
[24] Kitchener outlined the arguments advanced in *Yr Arloeswr* in a letter (1951) to Aneirin Talfan Davies. (NLW, Aneirin Talfan Davies Collection).
[25] Unidentified and undated newspaper cutting in NLW, D. R. Davies Collection 40/2.
[26] Seamus Heaney, *The Redress of Poetry* (London: Faber, 1995), p. 160.
[27] Kitchener Davies advances this reading of the Welsh drama tradition in several places, including scripts of the BBC Wales programmes entitled *Y Ddrama Gymraeg*. The quotation from Saunders Lewis is taken from this source.
[28] This passage appears in brackets in the text of 'Adfyw' that is printed in *Poetry Wales*, but is set as a separate paragraph in the script as broadcast (NLW, BBC, Box 31).
[29] The phrase comes from the letter (December 1939) written by three psychiatrists to the *British Medical Journal* explaining why 'the evacuation of small children between the ages of two and five introduces major psychological problems'. See Adam Phillips, *Winnicott* (London: Faber, 1988), Chapter 3. For the discussion that here follows I am indebted to John Bowlby, *Loss* (London: Penguin edition, 1986).
[30] Susan Sontag, *Illness as Metaphor* (Harmondsworth: Penguin, 1983), p. 27.

Select Bibliography

James Kitchener Davies

Collected works

Davies, Mair I. (gol.), *Gwaith James Kitchener Davies* (Llandysul: Gomer, 1980).

Thomas, M. Wynn and Manon Rhys (goln.), *James Kitchener Davies: Detholiad o'i Waith* [*JKDDW*] (Caerdydd: Gwasg Prifysgol Cymru, 2002).

Other published work

'Fy llong fach', *Western Mail* (19 September 1925).

'Drychiolaeth', *The Dragon* (May 1926), 165.

'Cyflwr Cwm Rhondda', *Efrydydd* IV, 8 (1928), 232–5 (now reprinted in *JKDDW*).

'Drwy fwg baco' (Y seiat rydd), *Efrydydd* IV, 10 (Gorffennaf 1928), 273–5.

'Y staff ysgol' (Y seiat rydd), *Efrydydd* VI, 3 (Rhagfyr 1929), 58–9.

'Arwydd y Grog', *Efrydydd* VII, 9 (Mehefin 1931), 240–6 (now reprinted in *JKDDW*).

'Some impressions of Bryn Mawr', *Welsh Nationalist* I, 9 (September 1932), 6.

'Thoughts after an election', *Welsh Nationalist* II, 4 (April 1933), 7 (now reprinted in *JKDDW*).

'Diarfogi: y cam nesaf: cyfraniad Prydain', *Efrydydd* IX, 10 (Gorffennaf 1933), 275–8.

'Heddychu yn Rhydychen', *Efrydydd* X, 1 (Hydref 1933), 26–8.

'Y Llysfam: stori fer', *Y Ford Gron* (Medi 1933), 251, 262, 264 (now reprinted in *JKDDW*).

'Drama fawr Gymraeg: pam na ddaeth eto', *Y Ford Gron* IV (1934), 176, 192 (now reprinted in *JKDDW*).

'Cynhadledd Caer Urdd y Deyrnas: llunio "Cymdogaeth"', *Efrydydd* X, 8 (Mai 1935), 220–3 (now reprinted in *JKDDW*).

'This year's new plays', *News Chronicle* (18 October 1935).

'Pitfall for amateur players', *News Chronicle* (25 October 1935).

'Salaries for actors', *News Chronicle* (1 November 1935).

'Choice of play for the Club Room', *News Chronicle* (8 November 1935).
'They act on business lines', *News Chronicle* (6 December 1935).
'Rhondda Roundabout on the air', *News Chronicle* (13 December 1935).
'Plays inspired by the *News Chronicle*', *News Chronicle* (20 December 1935).
'Fine lead for school producers', *News Chronicle* (27 December 1935).
'Will 1936 produce the great playwright?', *News Chronicle* (3 January 1936).
'Competition prizes and royalties', *News Chronicle* (10 January 1936).
'Girl students on the air', *News Chronicle* (17 January 1936).
'Child-heroes absent from our stage', *News Chronicle* (24 January 1936).
'Footlights on the Celtic Twilight', *News Chronicle* (31 January 1936).
'Welsh plays and London theatre', *News Chronicle* (7 February 1936).
'Dialects problem on the Welsh stage', *News Chronicle* (14 February 1936) (now reprinted in *JKDDW*).
'The radio wants pioneers', *News Chronicle* (28 February 1936).
'Economic value', *Western Mail* (29 February 1936).
'The sign of the Cross through the ages', *Western Mail* (11 April 1936).
'Gweled fy enw yn y llaid. Ac mewn print – ', *Western Mail* (30 August 1936).
'Codi craith ar bren a chalon', *Western Mail* (15 October 1936) (now reprinted in *JKDDW*).
'Lle Cymru yng nghynllwynion Lloegr', *Heddiw* 1, 3 (Hydref 1936), 90–2 (now reprinted in *JKDDW*).
'An analysis of present day Welsh literary effort', *Western Mail* (17 October 1936).
'Fy awr gydag Edward Frenin', *Western Mail* (19 November 1936) (now reprinted in *JKDDW*).
'Cyfaredd diwrnod lladd mochyn', *Western Mail* (18 January 1937) (now reprinted in *JKDDW*).
'Cenedlaetholdeb Cymru a chomiwnyddiaeth', *Heddiw* (Ebrill 1937), 84–90 (now reprinted in *JKDDW*).
'Enwau soniarus a dieithr', *Western Mail* (30 June 1937) (now reprinted in *JKDDW*).
'Rhwng Aeron a Theifi – yno y mae haf', *Western Mail* (17 August 1937) (now reprinted in *JKDDW*).
'Gwasg rydd Lloegr' (Senedd y Llan I), *Y Ddraig Goch* (Ionawr 1938), 2–4.
'Chwyldro' (Senedd y Llan II), *Y Ddraig Goch* (Chwefror 1938), 2.
'Boneddigion sy'n eistedd yn Llundain', *Y Ddraig Goch* (Mehefin 1938), 2.

'Yr eisteddfod a'r ddrama', *Heddiw* 5, 4 (Awst 1939), 170–9 (now reprinted in *JKDDW*).
'Coupons in Welsh', Letter, *Western Mail* (15 January 1942).
'Welsh in schools', Letter, *Western Mail* (23 August 1943).
Adjudication of Long Play competition, *Cyfansoddiadau a Beirniadaethau: Eisteddfod Genedlaethol Bangor, 1943* (Liverpool: Hugh Evans, n.d.), pp. 178–84.
'Ledled Cymru', *Y Faner* (23 Awst 1944).
'Athrawon ar gynghorau lleol', *Yr Athro* (Medi–Rhagfyr 1945), 85.
'Dadl economaidd Plaid Cymru', in J. Gwyn Griffiths (ed.), *Wedi'r Ddarlith – Casgliad o Ysgrifau gan fyfyrwyr a chyn-fyfyrwyr* (Caernarfon, 1945), pp. 9–13.
Complete text of letter to Mary Lewis about 1945 production of *Meini Gwagedd*, in D. Jacob Davies, 'Llwyfannu Meini Gwagedd', *Y Genhinen* IV, 217–22 (now reprinted in *JKDDW*).
'New education bill', Letter, *Western Mail* (11 February 1946).
'Welsh Member's speech', Letter, *Western Mail* (26 July 1946).
'Dangerous political doctrine', Letter, *Western Mail* (27 August 1946).
'Ing Cenhedloedd', *Y Fflam* 1, 1 (Nadolig 1946), 43–50.
'Tir ei geraint, Tregaron', *Y Ddraig Goch* (Tachwedd 1947) (now reprinted in *JKDDW*).
Review of Ieuan Griffiths's farce, *Tarfu'r C'lomennod*, *Y Fflam* 5 (Mai 1948), 55–6.
'Drama a beirniadaeth lenyddol', *The Torch* 2 (Spring 1949), 13–16 (now reprinted in *JKDDW*).
'Beirdd i'r theatr', *Lleufer* (Haf 1950), 59–64 (now reprinted in *JKDDW*).
'Saunders Lewis a'r ddrama Gymraeg', in Pennar Davies (gol.), *Saunders Lewis, ei Feddwl a'i Waith* (Dinbych: Gee, 1950), pp. 90–120 (now reprinted in *JKDDW*).
'Hen athro, gan dri o ysgol Dregaron', *Llafar* (1951) (Llandysul: Gomer, 1952), 70–2.
'Poet's view', *Herald of Wales* (1 December 1951), 7 (now reprinted in *JKDDW*).
'Welsh language: our defence consolidated – now must advance', *Herald of Wales* (8 December 1951), 1 and 7 (now reprinted in *JKDDW*).
'Hall-marked', *Herald of Wales* (15 December 1951).
'A forgotten school of Welsh dramatists', *Herald of Wales* (22 December 1951).
'Gweddi': section of *Sŵn y Gwynt sy'n Chwythu* published in *Llafar* (Llandysul: Gomer, 1953), 71–2.

'Adfyw', in *Y Cardi* 3 (Awst 1968), 160–1.
'Nunc Dimittis . . .', *Poetry Wales* (Winter 1982), 32 (now reprinted in *JKDDW*).
'Le Bon Dieu est Mort', *Poetry Wales* (Winter 1982), 35 (now reprinted in *JKDDW*).
'Adfyw', *Poetry Wales* (Winter 1982), 20–4 (now reprinted as Adfyw 2 in *JKDDW*).
'F'annwyl Mrs Lewis', extract from letter about staging *Meini Gwagedd*, *Poetry Wales* (Winter 1982), 25–6.
'An analysis of present day Welsh literary effort', reprinted from *Western Mail* (17 October 1936), in *Poetry Wales* (Winter 1982), 27–33.

Translation
Hen Wlad fy Nhadau (Translation of Jack Jones, *Land of my Fathers*), Welsh Drama Series No.128 (n.d., 1938) (London: Samuel French and Co.).

BBC materials (National Library of Wales)
'*Y Pentref*: 1. Y Farchnad a'r Mart', 14 January 1943 (BBC, Box 167).
(With Iorwerth Peate): '*Y Pentref*: 5. Crefftwyr y Pentref', school broadcast, 3 June 1943 (BBC, Box 167).
Gloria in Excelsis. Play for children. *Children's Hour*, 19 December 1944 (BBC, Box 142).
Review of two plays and two stories for children. *Children's Hour Talk*, 30 April 1946 (BBC, Box 112).
Meini Gwagedd, edited version, 21 June 1946 (BBC, Box 45).
Y Ddrama Gymraeg. Chairing discussion, 7, 14, 21, 28 March and 3 April 1947 (BBC, Box 97).
'Y Saer', school broadcast, 28 October 1947 (BBC, Box 169).
'Y Crydd', school broadcast, 4 November 1947 (BBC, Box 169).
'Y Gof', school broadcast, 11 November 1947 (BBC, Box 169).
Cwm Glo, abridged version, 28 September 1950 (BBC, Box 52).
'Adfyw', broadcast script different from printed version, 14 September 1950 (BBC, Box 31) (now reprinted as Adfyw 1 in *JKDDW*).

Other unpublished materials
Miss Blodeuwedd (holograph drama in B. J. Morse papers; University of Wales, Cardiff, 3/146).
'Sacrament' and 'O Bridd y Ddaear' (holograph poems in B. J. Morse papers; University of Wales, Cardiff, 3/146) (now published in *JKDDW*).

Unpublished letters

28 September 1927: Letter to T. Gwynn Jones requesting help in placing Ben Bowen in context of Welsh poetic tradition (N[ational] L[ibrary] of W[ales]: T. Gwynn Jones papers).

27 October 1930: Letter to T. Gwynn Jones about interest in writing play on the Departure of Arthur (NLW: T. Gwynn Jones papers).

30 October 1932: Letter to Selwyn Jones, expressing interest in staging of *Adar y To* by the 'Celtiaid', but requesting three weeks for revision of the text (NLW: Selwyn Jones papers, 95/2).

31 August 1934: Letter to D. R. Davies about rumour of Hollywood interest in *Cwm Glo* (NLW: D. R. Davies papers, 40/1).

12 August 1943: Letter about *Adfeilion* to editors of *Y Dryw* series (NLW: Alwyn D. Rees papers, C5/2).

29 November 1948: Letter to Dr Noelle Davies about a piece on the Coal Board in south Wales in *Sunday Observer* (NLW: Dr Noelle Davies papers, 12 (19)).

1951: Letter to Aneirin Talfan Davies, from East Glamorgan Hospital, Church Village, about contribution to a series of radio poems (NLW: Aneirin Talfan Davies papers).

20 March 1952: Letter to Wil Ifan, from East Glamorgan Hospital, Church Village, thanking him for a kind financial gesture (NLW: Wil Ifan papers, 164).

Reviews, articles and critical studies

Aaron, Wil, producer of *Almanac* programme on Kitchener Davies (S4C, 1982).

Anon, 'Pryddest yn olyniaeth Pantycelyn', *Y Tyst* (Hydref 1953).

Ashton, G. M., '*Cwm Glo*', *Tir Newydd* (Haf 1936), 2–3.

Davies, Aneirin Talfan, 'Y Gwynt sy'n Chwythu', *Western Mail* (6 July 1974).

Davies, D. Jacob, 'O Nyth y Frân', *Y Cymro* (29 Medi 1956).

Davies, D. Jacob, 'Llwyfannu *Meini Gwagedd*', *Y Genhinen* IV, 217–22.

Davies, David, 'An appreciation', *Welsh Nation* (September 1952), 3.

Davies, Eic, 'Kitchener', *Y Ddraig Goch* (Hydref 1952).

Davies, Menna, *Traddodiad Llenyddol y Rhondda* (Ph.D., University of Wales, Cardiff, 1981).

Davies, Pennar, 'Gwaith James Kitchener Davies', *Poetry Wales* (Winter 1982), 36–40.

Davies, Pennar, *Dock Leaves* 5, 15 (Winter 1954).

Edwards, H. W. J., 'An appreciation', *Herald of Wales* (30 August 1952).
Edwards, H. W. J., 'The Story of Man', *Herald of Wales* (28 March 1953).
Griffiths, J. Gwyn, 'Testament olaf Kitchener Davies', *Y Dysgedydd* CXXXIV (4 Ebrill 1954), 94.
H.M., Review of *Susanna*, *Heddiw* (Hydref 1938), 60.
Hughes, N. Cadvan, '*Meini Gwagedd*', *Lleufer* IV (1948), 49.
Jenkins, Kathryn, '"O Lwynpiod i Lwynpia": hunangofiant James Kitchener Davies', *Ysgrifau Beirniadol* XIX (Dinbych: Gee, 1993).
Jones, Bobi, 'Awel euog Kitchener Davies', *Barn* 46 (Awst, 1966), 272–3.
Jones, D. Lloyd, 'Ovation for verse play experiment', *Western Mail* (15 May 1945).
Jones, D. Lloyd, 'Drama arwyddocaol. Perfformio *Meini Gwagedd*', *Y Faner* (23 Mai 1945).
Jones, Gwilym R., 'Canu James Kitchener Davies', *Y Faner* (22 Gorffennaf 1953).
Jones, Gwilym R., 'Bardd-Ddramawr o Geredigion', *Barn* (Hydref 1980), 223.
Jones, T. James, 'Gweithiau Kitchener Davies', *Y Faner* (29 Awst 1980), 10.
Lewis, D. Haydn, 'Wedi tymor o amser', *Y Faner* (Ebrill 1966), 160.
Lewis, J. Saunders, Adjudication of *Meini Gwagedd, Cyfansoddiadau a Beirniadaethau Eisteddfod Genedlaethol Llandybïe, 1944* (National Eisteddfod, Llandybïe, 1944), pp. 98–100.
Lewis, J. Saunders, 'Pryddest Kitchener Davies', *Y Faner* (21 Hydref 1953).
Lewis, J. Saunders, 'Pryddest Kitchener Davies', *Seren* (23 Rhagfyr 1953).
Llywelyn-Williams, Alun, Review of *Sŵn y Gwynt sy'n Chwythu*, *Lleufer* IX (1953), 170–2.
Morgan, D., 'Ffrwyth o ardd Kitchener Davies', *Lleufer* XXI, 24–8.
Parry, Thomas, 'Drama fel llenyddiaeth', *Y Traethodydd* 3, XX (1952), 122.
Roberts, Kate, 'Marw dramawr', *Y Faner* (27 Hydref 1952).
Rowlands, John and Glyn Jones (eds.), *Profiles* (Llandysul: Gomer, 1980).
Rhys, Prosser, '*Meini Gwagedd*', *Y Faner* (23 Awst 1944).
Samuel, Wynne, 'Kitchener Davies ar y bocs sebon', *Y Ddraig Goch* (Hydref/Tachwedd 1980), 6–7.
Thomas, M. Wynn, 'Keeping the Rhondda for Wales: the case of J. Kitchener Davies', *Transactions of the Honourable Society of Cymmrodorion* 26 (2000), 119–34.
Wil Ifan, 'Keeping a promise to oneself', *Western Mail* (2 September 1952).

Williams, D. J., 'Gair o goffa', *Y Ddraig Goch* (Medi 1952), 172.
Williams, D. Matthew, Adjudication on *Meini Gwagedd, Cyfansoddiadau a Beirniadaethau Eisteddfod Genedlaethol Llandybïe, 1944* (National Eisteddfod, Llandybïe, 1944), pp. 175–9.
Williams, I. M., 'The special function', *Planet* 30 (1976), 44–50.
Williams, I. M., 'Two Welsh poets', *Poetry Wales* (Spring 1981), 104.
Williams, I. M., 'Treiddier trwy bob newid', *Poetry Wales* (Winter 1982), 40–57.
Williams, I. M., *Kitchener Davies* (Caernarfon: Pantycelyn, 1984).
Williams, Loreen, 'Portread y mis: Tish Harcombe', *Tafod Elai* (Hydref 1988), 8–9.
Williams, Rhydwen, 'James Kitchener Davies', *Poetry Wales* (Winter 1982), 58–63.
Williams, Tim, 'The metaphysic of the text: a consumer's guide to *Sŵn y Gwynt*', *Poetry Wales* (Winter 1982), 65–75.
Wyn, Ieuan, 'Y Llenor', *Y Ddraig Goch* (Hydref/Tachwedd 1980), 6.

Articles and reviews on the *Cwm Glo* controversy

'Cerddetwr' (David Griffiths), *The Amman Valley Chronicle* (17 January 1935), 2.
'Cerddetwr' (David Griffiths), *The Amman Valley Chronicle* (14 February 1935), 2.
'Cerddetwr' (David Griffiths), *The Amman Valley Chronicle* (21 March 1935), 2.
'Cerddetwr' (David Griffiths), *The Amman Valley Chronicle* (24 October 1935), 2.
'Cerddetwr' (David Griffiths), *The Amman Valley Chronicle* (19 December 1935), 2.
'Cerddetwr' (David Griffiths), *The Amman Valley Chronicle* (2 January 1936), 2.
Edwards, Hywel Teifi, 'Nid bachan budr yw Dai', in *Arwr Glew Erwau'r Glo* (Llandysul: Gomer, 1994), pp. 143–212.
Etheridge, Ken, '*Cwm Glo*: a modern morality', *The Amman Valley Chronicle* (14 February 1935), 5.
'G', *The Amman Valley Chronicle* (2 January 1936), 4.
'Gwaencaugurwen and Brynamman notes', *The Amman Valley Chronicle* (21 November 1935), 3.
Rhys, Manon, 'Atgyfodi *Cwm Glo* Kitchener Davies', in Hywel Teifi Edwards (ed.), *Cwm Rhondda* (Llandysul: Gomer, 1995), pp. 276–300.

Relevant materials from National Library of Wales

Letter from Saunders Lewis about *Meini Gwagedd* (2 September 1944) (copy in Thomas Parry-Williams papers, Ch723) (now published in *JKDDW*).
Letter from Percy Griffiths to Kate Roberts (22 December 1938) (Kate Roberts papers, 1B).
Y Gŵr Bendigaid (Rhydwen Williams papers, 56).
Election leaflets from Rhondda (Ivor T. Rees, 14).

Important sources of biographical information

Llwyd, Rheinallt, taped interview with Letitia (Tish) Harcombe, 17 August 1989.
Thomas, M. Wynn, interview with Glyn James, 24 February 2000.

Translations

Clancy, Joseph P., 'The Sound of the Wind that is Blowing', in *Twentieth Century Welsh Poems* (Llandysul: Gomer, 1982), pp. 109–19.

Index

Note: page references in italic refer to illustrations.

Aberaeron 50
Aberystwyth *see* University College of Wales
'Absalom and Achitophel' (John Dryden) 86
Act of Union 42
Adar y To 32
Adfeilion 62
'Adfyw' 4–5, 15, 21, 27, 80, 84, 90–3
Aeron 50, 52, 53, 70, 89
Amanwy 33
amateur drama 37–8
American Wales 23
Amlyn ac Amig (J. Saunders Lewis) 75, 79–80
'Analysis of present day Welsh literary effort, An' 39–40
Ancient Mariner ('The Rime of the Ancient Mariner', Samuel Taylor Coleridge) 56
anglicization 3
Anglicanism 9, 11
Ann's screech 5, 10, 50, 57
anti-colonialism 14, 17
anti-war sentiments 43
Arloeswr, Yr 64–6, 75
Arthur 42
'Arwydd y Grog' 28
Athro, Yr 20
Auden, W. H. 46

Baldwin, Stanley 30
Banbury 6, 8, 82
Bardsey Island 28
Barth, Karl 62, 79
BBC Welsh Region Radio 32
Beckett, Samuel 56
Bedwyr (Bedivere) 42–3
Berdyaev, Nicholas 62
Berry, R. G. 37

Blaengarw 6–7, 14
Blaengwynfi Primary School 23
Blodeuwedd (Saunders Lewis) 49
Bodo Mari 6, 8, 10, 14, 23, 35, 81–2
Bottomley, Gordon 46
Boudicca 43
Bowen, Ben 29–30
Bruch, Max 59
Buchedd Garmon (Saunders Lewis) 45, 49, 62
Bunyan, John 78
Bywyd a Marwolaeth Theomemphus (William Williams, Pantycelyn) 66, 77, 80–1

Calvinism 9, 12, 16, 63, 65
Cambrian Combine Strike 6
cancer 72, 82
capitalism 27, 29, 31, 67
cattle trail 6–7
Central Labour College, London 19
Change (J. O. Francis) 31, 38
Chesterton, G. K. 62
Children's Hour (*Awr y Plant*) 53, 57
Christian faith 28, 43, 57, 63, 74–5
Clancy, Joseph P. 73, 75, 82
class issues 3
coalfield societies 2, 4, 7, 13–14
Cocktail Party, The (T. S. Eliot) 78
Cogito, ergo sum (René Descartes) 64
Coleridge, Samuel Taylor 56
communism 67
Conservatives 68–9
conversion, religious 80–2
Cook, Arthur J.
cross, sign of the 28
cultural colonization 11
Cwm Glo 2–3, 10, 30–3, 38, 41, 47, 48, 49, 51, 59, 60
'Cwm Rhondda' (Gwenallt) 89

104

'Cylch Cadwgan' 52
'Cymru 1937' (R. Williams Parry) 77
Cymru Fydd 25
Cynan (Albert Evans-Jones) 32, 41

Dallimore, Flo 51
Davies, Aneirin Talfan 75–6, 78, 79, 85
Davies, Cassie 10, 77
Davies, D. R. 60
Davies, D. T. 37, 48
Davies, Jacob 56
Davies, John Elwyn 59
Davies, George M. Ll. 24, 28
Davies, James Kitchener:
  Childhood experiences and Tregaron upbringing 1–6, 7; mother's death, and its influence 5–6, 35–6, 57, 64, 66, 81–5; father's influence 6–7, 83–4; move to Banbury 6; family 8, *9*, 71; chapel influence 9–10; education 11–14; father's remarriage 14; selling of Y Llain 14, 36, 65; stepmother 14–17, 36; move to Blaengarw 14; University College of Wales, Aberystwyth 17–20; teaching in Rhondda 20–2; involvement in peace movements 24–5; soap-box speaking and electioneering 26–7; faith 28; teaching Welsh 29; publication of *Cwm Glo* and reactions 30–4; the Pandy Players and amateur drama *30*, 34–8; Welsh-language theatre 38–9; the issue of realism in Welsh drama 39–41; historical writing 41–3; influence of events at Penyberth 44–5; influence of T. S. Eliot 46, 78; marriage to Mair Rees *51*, 50–2; 'Cylch Cadwgan' 52–3; publication of *Meini Gwagedd* and reactions 54–63; performance of *Meini Gwagedd* in Lampeter 59–61; *Ing Cenhedloedd* 63; *Yr Arloeswr* 64–5; election campaigning 67–9, *91*; campaign to establish Welsh-medium schools 69–70; struggle with War Office 71–2; cancer 72–3; publication of *Sŵn y Gwynt sy'n Chwythu* and reactions 73–7; *Amlyn ac Amig* 79–80; 'Adfyw' 81–5, 92; death 86–7; tributes and the making of a legend 88–90; fire of 1990 90
Davies, Letitia (sister) *8*, 8, 14, 34–5, 71, 84
Davies, Pennar 89
Davies, Tegla 78
Davies, Thomas (brother) *8*, 8, 14, 84
Davies, Thomas (father) 6–7, 14–16, 36, *51*, 83–4
Dawson, Christopher 62
Ddraig Goch, Y 28
Ddrama Gymraeg, Y 77, 78
death 85, 88
debates, school 13
'Deluge, 1939, The' (Saunders Lewis) 27
Descartes, René 64
dialect 5, 10, 36–7, 39, 59, 76
'Dialects Problem on the Welsh Stage' 5
Dies Irae 43–4
disarmament 24
Dock Leaves 88
Dryden, John 85

'Easter 1916' (W. B. Yeats) 88–9
East Glamorgan Hospital, Church Village 72
economic circumstances 6
education 11–12, 14
Education Act, 1944 69
Edwards, H. W. J. 68–9
Edwards, J. M. 76
Edwards, Meredith 38
Edwards, O. M. 13
Efrydydd, Yr 24, 34
Eisteddfod Genedlaethol (National Eisteddfod) 30, 32, 48, 49, 53–4, 57, 64, 68, 76
election campaigning 26, 67–8
Eliot, T. S. 46, 77, 78–9
Elphin (Robert Arthur Griffith) 49
England 6, 23, 42, 44
English language 11
'Enwau Soniarus a Dieithr' 29
Eosiaid, Yr (Idwal Jones) 19
Etheridge, Ken 33
Evans, Caradoc 33

Evans, Clifford 38
Evans, William *see* Wil Ifan
Evans-Jones, Albert *see* Cynan
exile 6, 15

faith *see* Christian faith
Faner, Y (Baner ac Amserau Cymru) 58
fate 62–3
father *see* Davies, Thomas
Family Reunion, The (T. S. Eliot) 46, 78, 84–5
Ffynhonnau (Rhydwen Williams) 89
'Fine Lead for School Producers' 11
fire (1990) 90
Flecker, James Elroy 46
'Footlights on the Celtic Stage' 47
Four Quartets (T. S. Eliot) 78
Francis, J. O. 17, 31, 38, 49
free will 62–3
Freud, Sigmund 80
From Reparation to Industrial Ruin (George M. Ll. Davies) 24
'Fy Awr gydag Edward Frenin' 6

gardening 70–1, 82
Garthewin 60
Gate Theatre 60
General Strike, 1926 23
Gloria in Excelsis 57
God 63, 65–6, 74, 80
Griffiths, David *see* Amanwy
Griffiths, J. Gwyn 52
Griffiths, Robert Arthur *see* Elphin
Gruffydd, Dafydd 56
Gruffydd, W. J. 37, 78
Gwenallt (David James (Gwenallt) Jones) 88, 89

'Hallmarked' 3
Hanes Llenyddiaeth Gymraeg (Thomas Parry) 48
Hardy, Thomas 47
Harris, Howell 12
Heaney, Seamus 10, 72
Heddiw 27, 34, 44, 48
Hen Wlad fy Nhadau 48
Herald of Wales, The 4, 70, 76
historical drama 48–9
Horner, Arthur 23

Howell of Gwent (J. O. Francis) 49
Hwb i'r Galon (Cassie Davies) 10

Ibsen, Henrik 37, 58
Informer, The 34
Ing Cenhedloedd 63–4, 67, 75
Introduction to the Psychology of Religion, An (Robert H. Thouless) 80
Ireland 25, 54

Jones, David James (Gwenallt) *see* Gwenallt
Jones, Emrys 8
Jones, Idwal 19–20
Jones, Jack 48, 49
Jones, T. Gwynn 18–9, 23, 43
Jones, T. James 89
Jones, Thomas 12–13

Kavanagh, Patrick 54
Keynes, J. M. 23
kinship ties 8
Kitch (James Kitchener Davies) 8–9
Kitch (musical) 1, 89
'Kitch' (Rhydwen Williams) 88
Kitchener, Lord 8–9

Labour Party 23, 67–8
Lacey, Jack 53
Lampeter 19, 58–61
Land of My Fathers (Jack Jones) 48–9
language 5, 56
language games 10
Lawrence, D. H. 34
Lewis, J. Saunders 27, 32, 34, 36, 38, 41, 44–6, 48, 49, 58, 60, 75, 77, 78–9, 80–1, 87–8
Lewis, Mary 59–61
'Little Gidding' (T. S. Eliot) 78
Llain, Y 2, 8, 9, 14, 16, 36, 65, 71, 80, 84, 86, 92
Llandybïe 53–4
Llethr Ddu 90–1, 93
Llwch (T. James Jones) 89–90
Llwynpiod 6, 9, 80, 92
'Llysfam, Y' 14–17, 35, 36, 51, 57, 84
London 7, 60

MacNeice, Louis 46

Maerdy 26
Mainwaring, W. J. 67
Maritain, Jacques 62
Marquand, Hilary 23
marriage 51, 51–2, 82
Meini Gwagedd 2–3, 10, 38, 40, 46, 54–6, 67, 70, 84–5
Methodists 1, 9, 47, 80
miners' General Strike 23
Miners' Next Step, The 25
Miss Blodeuwedd 49–51
modernism 52
Monica (J. Saunders Lewis) 34
morality play 77–8, 79
Morris-Jones, John 18
Mossbawn (Seamus Heaney) 10
mother 5–6, 11, 14, 16, 35, 36, 57, 64, 81–3, 84
Mrs Warren's Profession (George Bernard Shaw) 31
Murder in the Cathedral (T. S. Eliot) 46, 78–9
'My Country the Worst Hell in Europe Today' (J. Saunders Lewis) 27, 32, 36

National Pageant of Wales, The 41
National Peace Council 24
nationalism 17, 19
News Chronicle, The 33, 38, 40, 42, 48
Niebuhr, Reinhold 62
Nonconformism 19
'Nunc Dimittis' 50

O'Casey, Sean 38
O'Flaherty, Liam 34
Oxford 24

pacifism 12, 17, 24, 52
Pandy Players, the 30, 34, 41, 51, 70
Parry, R. Williams 77
Parry, Thomas 48, 79
Parry-Williams, T. H. 17, 18–19, 77
Peace Society 72
Peace Vote 24
Peate, Iorwerth 13, 42, 53
Pentre Secondary School 52
Penyberth 27, 44–5
Phillips, Stephen 46
Pilgrim's Progress (John Bunyan) 78

pit work 14, 17
Plaid Cymru (Plaid Genedlaethol Cymru) 13, 25, 27, 32, 33, 42, 44–5, 67–8, 89
plays, school 13
poetry 55, 57–60, 63, 64, 75–6, 80
Poetry Wales 52
Pollitt, Harry 26
Porth 27, 52
Powell, S. M. 11–13
printed word 10
Pritchard, T. J. Llywelyn 12
Purgatory (W. B. Yeats) 58

Quite Early One Morning (Dylan Thomas) 76

radio 37, 56, 75–6, 78, 90–1
realism 39–40, 48–9, 59
Rees, Alwyn D. 62
Rees, Mair (wife) 50–1
Rhondda 2–3, 6, 8, 19, 20–1, 23–4, 26, 29, 30–1, 47, 50, 53, 61, 67–8, 69, 71, 74, 86, 90–2
'Rhys, Dafydd' (*nom de plume*) 50
Rhys, Manon (daughter) 89–90
Rhys, Prosser 58
Richard, Henry 1, 12, 72
Roberts, Kate 25, 26, 88
Rowland, Daniel 12
rural life 5, 7, 53, 61–2

Samuel, Wynne 26
Sayers, Dorothy L. 46
seiat 81
'Senedd y Llan' 28
sentimentality 52–3, 59, 85
Shakespeare, William 76
Shaw, George Bernard 31
Shelley, Percy Bysshe 77
Sinn Fein 17
soap box 26
socialism 27–8
socio-geography 13–14
Sontag, Susan 82
south Wales 7, 14, 16
Spengler, Oswald 62
'Staff ysgol' 19–20
stepmother 14–17, 35, 51

Stowe, Harriet Beecher 12
Strata Florida 72
summer schools 25
Sunday school 9
Susanna 46–7, 51
Swansea Welsh Drama Company 33, 34
Sŵn y Gwynt sy'n Chwythu 2–3, 11, 29, 40, 46, 47, 56, 66, 67, 70, 72–5, 77–9, 80–5, 86–7, 89, 90
Synge, John Millington 38

teacher training 17
teaching 20, 52, 70
Thomas, Clydach 34
Thomas, Dylan 76, 88
Thomas, Edward 56–7
Thomas, Gwyn 27
Thomas, Iorwerth (Iorrie) 68
Thomas, Rachel 38
Thouless, Robert H. 80
Three Wayfarers, The (Thomas Hardy) 47
Tonypandy 14, 51, 92
Torch, The 18
translation 47–8
Trawsfynydd 72
Trealaw 1, 28, 52, 68, 71
Tregaron 1–5, 6–7, 9–10, 11–13, 14, 36, 50, 58, 63, 68, 71–2, 86, 90
Tregaron County School 11, 17, 77
tributes 89–90
Tri Dyn Dieithr, Y 47
Twm o'r Nant 77
Twm Siôn Catti 12, 47

Uncle Tom's Cabin (Harriet Beecher Stowe) 12
Under Milk Wood (Dylan Thomas) 76
University College of Wales, Aberystwyth 17
University College of Wales, Aberystwyth Drama Movement 17

Urdd y Deyrnas 24, 25

Valentine, Lewis 27
Versailles Treaty 24

'Wales's place in England's conspiracies' ('Lle Cymru yng nghynllwynion Lloegr') 44
War Office 71–2
Welsh language 3, 6, 11, 18, 29, 39, 53, 62, 67, 69–70, 72, 89
Welsh literary tradition 18
Welsh Nation, The 26
Welsh Outlook, The (D. T. Davies) 48
Welsh-medium education 69–70, 89
Wil Ifan (William Evans) 85
'Will 1936 Produce the Great Welsh Playwright?' 40–2
Williams, Charles 46
Williams, D. J. 17, 27, 90
Williams, D. Matthew 58
Williams, Emlyn
Williams, Ifor 18
Williams, John Ellis 42, 78
Williams, Llywelyn 49
Williams, Morris 25
Williams Pantycelyn (Saunders Lewis) 80–1
Williams, Pantycelyn, William 12, 64, 66, 77, 80–1
Williams, R. R. 29
Williams, Rhydwen 52, 85, 88, 89
World Disarmament Conference 24–5
World War, First 3, 14, 18–19
World War, Second 52–3, 63, 67

Yeats, W. B. 38, 58, 73, 88–9
Ymadawiad Arthur (T. Gwynn Jones) 23, 43
Ynys Afallon 42–4

Zeldin, Theodore 90
Zimmern, Alfred 23